THE FILE

A PERSONAL HISTORY

Timothy Garton Ash

Atlantic Books
LONDON

First published in Great Britain in 1997 by HarperCollins*Publishers*.

This revised edition published in Great Britain in 2009 by Atlantic Books, an imprint of Grove Atlantic Ltd.

9 10

A CIP catalogue record for this book is available
from the British Library.

ISBN: 978 1 84887 088 8

Printed in Great Britain

Atlantic Books
An imprint of Grove Atlantic Ltd
Ormond House
26–27 Boswell Street
London
WC1N 3JZ

www.atlantic-books.co.uk

For D., T. and A.

A Note on Names

The following names in the text are pseudonyms: Andrea, Claudia, Flash Harry, Frau Duncker and Frau R. Three informers are identified only by their Stasi aliases: 'Michaela', 'Schuldt' and 'Smith'. If anyone might be tempted to expose the real people behind these names – which in several cases would not be difficult – I would ask them to refrain from doing so, for reasons that should become clear.

'*GUTEN TAG,*' says bustling Frau Schulz, 'you have a very interesting file.' And there it is, a buff-coloured binder, some two inches thick, rubber-stamped on the front cover: *OPK-Akte, MfS, XV2889/81.* Underneath is written, in a neat, clerical hand: „Romeo".

Romeo?

'Yes, that was your code-name', says Frau Schulz, and giggles.

I SIT DOWN at a small plastic-wood table in Frau Schulz's cramped room in the Federal Authority for the Records of the State Security Service of the former German Democratic Republic: the ministry of the files. As I open the binder, I find myself thinking of an odd moment in my East German life.

One night in 1980, when I was living as a student in East Berlin, I came back with a girlfriend to my room in a crumbling Wilhelmine tenement house in the borough of Prenzlauer Berg. This was a room with a view – a view into it. Large french windows gave directly on to a balcony and, were it not for the net curtains, people living across the street could look straight in.

As we embraced on the narrow bed, Andrea suddenly pulled away, finished undressing, went over to the window and threw open the net curtains. She turned on the glaring main light and then came back to me. Had this been, say, Oxford, I might have been a little surprised about the bright light and the open curtains. But this was Berlin, so I thought no more about it.

Until, that is, I learned about the file. Then I remembered this moment and started wondering whether Andrea had been working for the Stasi, and whether she had opened the curtains so we could be photographed from the other side of the street.

Perhaps those photographs are lurking in this binder, which Frau Schulz has already inspected. What was it she said? 'You have a very interesting file.'

Hastily turning the pages, I'm relieved to find that there are no such photographs here and that Andrea does not appear as an informer. But there are other things that touch me.

Here, for example, is an observation report describing a visit I apparently paid to East Berlin on 06.10.79 from 16.07 hours to 23.55 hours. The alias given me by the Stasi at this date was, less romantically, '246816'.

16.07 hours
'246816' was taken up for observation after leaving the Bahnhof Friedrichstrasse frontier crossing. The person to be observed went to the newspaper stand in the upper station concourse and bought a 'Freie Welt', a 'Neues Deutschland' and a 'Berliner Zeitung'. Then the object [that's me] walked questingly around the station.

16.15 hours
in the upper station concourse '246816' greeted a female person with handshake and kiss on the cheek. This female person received the code-name 'Beret'. 'Beret' carried a dark brown shoulder bag. Both left the station and went, conversing, to the Berliner Ensemble on Brechtplatz.

16.25 hours
both entered the restaurant
    Ganymed
    Berlin-Mitte
    Am Schiffbauerdamm

After *c.* 2 minutes the persons to be observed left the restaurant and went via Friedrichstrasse and Unter den Linden to the Operncafé.

16.52 hours
'246816' and 'Beret' entered the restaurant
  Operncafé
  Berlin-Mitte
  Unter den Linden
They took seats in the café and drank coffee.

18.45 hours
they left the café and went to Bebelplatz. In the time from

18.45 hours
until

20.40 hours
they both watched with interest the torchlit procession to honour the 30th anniversary of the GDR. Thereafter '246816' and 'Beret' went along the street Unter den Linden [and] Friedrichstrasse to the street Am Schiffbauerdamm.

21.10 hours
they entered there the restaurant Ganymed. In the restaurant they were not under observation.

23.50 hours
both left the gastronomic establishment and proceeded directly to the departure hall of the Bahnhof Friedrichstrasse frontier crossing, which they

23.55 hours
entered. 'Beret' was passed on to Main Department VI for documentation. The surveillance was terminated.

Person-description of object '246816'
  SEX: male
  AGE: 20–25 years
  HEIGHT: *c.* 1.75m

BUILD: slim
HAIR: dark blond
     short
DRESS: green jacket
     blue polo-neck pullover
     brown cord trousers

Person-description of connection 'Beret'
SEX: female
AGE: 30–35 years
HEIGHT: 1.75m–1.78m
BUILD: slim
HAIR: medium blonde
     curly
DRESS: dark blue cloth coat
     red beret
     blue jeans
     black boots
ACCESSORIES: dark brown handbag

I sit there, at the plastic-wood table, marvelling at this minutely detailed reconstruction of a day in my life and at the style that recalls a school exercise: never a sentence without a verb, the pretentious variation of 'gastronomic establishment'. I remember the slovenly gilt-and-red Ganymed, the plush Operncafé and the blue-shirted, pimpled youths in the thirtieth anniversary march-past, their paraffin-soaked torches trailing sparks in the misty night air. I smell again that peculiar East Berlin smell, a compound of the smoke from old-fashioned domestic boilers burning compressed coal-dust briquettes, exhaust fumes from the two-stroke engines of the little Trabant cars, cheap East European cigarettes, damp boots and sweat. But one thing I simply can't remember: who was she, my little red riding-hood? Or not so little: 1.75 – 1.78 metres, nearly my height. Slim, medium blonde, curly hair, 30–35, black boots? I sit there, under Frau Schulz's inquisitive eye, sensing an awful disloyalty to my own past.

Only when I get home, right home, to Oxford, do I find out who she was – by reading my own diary from that time. In fact, I discover the whole record of a short, intense, unhappy romance: of days and nights, of telephone calls and letters. Why, here at the back of the diary are two of her letters, carefully kept in their envelopes, with a postmark that says 'Post – so you keep in touch'. Folded inside one of the letters is a black-and-white photograph that she sent me when it was all over, to remember her by. Tousled hair, high cheekbones, a rather tense smile. How could I have forgotten?

My diary for that day in October 1979 has Claudia 'cheeky in red beret and blue uniform raincoat'. 'Over Friedrichstrasse,' it says, 'searched down to the soles of my shoes (Duckers. Officer very impressed.)' Now I remember how, at the underground checkpoint beneath the Friedrichstrasse railway station, a grey-uniformed officer took me into a curtained cubicle, made me empty the contents of my pockets on to a small table, examined each item minutely and even questioned me about individual entries in my pocket diary. He then ordered me to take off my heavy brown leather shoes, from Ducker & Son of Turl Street. Peering inside and then weighing them in his hand he said: 'Very good shoes.'

'Arm-in-arm, cheek-to-cheek w. Claudia to Operncafé', the diary goes on:

Becoming yet more intimate . . . The torchlit procession. The cold, cold east wind. Our warmth. The maze – encircled. Slipping through the columns, evading the policemen. Finally to 'Ganymed'. Tolerable dinner. C. re. her 'Jobben'. Her political activity. We cross back via Friedrichstr. To Diener's . . . c.0300 at Uhlandstr. Daniel, desperate and pale-faced before the flat door – locked out!

Daniel Johnson, son of the writer Paul Johnson, is today an established figure on *The Times*. He was then a fiercely intellectual Cambridge postgraduate, working on a doctorate about the history of German pessimism – of which he was always delighted to discover another specimen. We shared a spacious late nineteenth-century flat in the borough of Wilmersdorf, Uhlandstrasse 127. Daniel had forgotten his keys.

The 'maze' and 'columns' were, I presume, those of the regimented torch-bearing marchers of the Free German Youth, the gloriously misnamed communist youth organization. As for 'her political activity', Claudia belonged to the instantly recognizable generation of 1968. That evening she told me how they used to chant at the riot police a jingle which neatly captures the '68 mixture of political and sexual protest. In free translation it goes: 'Out here they are pigs/In bed they are figs.'

I last caught a glimpse of her, some time later, in the graveyard of the Berlin-Dahlem village church, at the funeral of the student leader Rudi Dutschke. She was still wearing her red beret. Or have I just imagined that final detail?

The Stasi's observation report, my diary entry: two versions of one day in a life. The 'object' described with the cold outward eye of the secret policeman and my own subjective, allusive, emotional self-description. But what a gift to memory is a Stasi file. Far better than Proust's madeleine.

I

THE 'OPK' ON THE FRONT COVER stands for *Operative
Personenkontrolle*, Operational Person Control. According to the
1985 edition of the *Dictionary of Political-Operational Work*, prepared by the Juridical Higher School of the Ministry for State
Security, an Operational Person Control was to identify anyone
who might have committed an offence according to the Criminal Code, or who might have a 'hostile-negative attitude', or
who might be exploited for hostile purposes by the enemy. The
central purpose of an OPK, the dictionary explains, is to answer
the question 'who's who?' Each file begins with an 'opening
report' and a 'plan of action'.

My opening report dates from March 1981. Prepared by one
Lieutenant Wendt, it gives my personal details, notes that I have
been studying in West Berlin since 1978, and lived from January
to June 1980 – actually it was October – in 'the capital of the
GDR'. (The authorities of the German Democratic Republic
always insisted on using this formula for East Berlin.) I travel
frequently from West Berlin to East Germany and Poland. I
have repeatedly 'made contact with operationally interesting
persons'. Consequently, 'there are grounds for suspecting that
G. [for Garton Ash, otherwise 'the object' or 'Romeo'] has
deliberately exploited his official functions as research student
and/or journalist to pursue intelligence activities'.

Lieutenant Wendt then reviews the information which
counter-intelligence department II/9 has pulled together for
this purpose from all the other departments of the Ministry.

Raw material follows later in the file: observation reports; summaries of intelligence from the files on my friend Werner Krätschell, a Protestant priest, and on the British Embassy; photocopies of articles I wrote about Poland for the West German news magazine *Der Spiegel*; copies of my own Polish notes and papers, photographed during a secret search of my luggage at Schönefeld airport, from where I was flying to Warsaw; even copies of the references written by my Oxford tutors for the British Council. In all, there are 325 pages.

Wendt's report pays special attention to information supplied by the Stasi's own informers, known as *Inoffizielle Mitarbeiter* – literally 'unofficial collaborators' – or IM for short. They were sub-divided into several categories: security, special, operative, conspirative, even the informer for running other informers. Since 1989, the initials IM have entered the German language. SS is the synonym in every European language for the loud, violent, outright bestiality of Nazism. IM has become, in German, the synonym for the routine, bureaucratic forms of infiltration, intimidation and collaboration which characterized the German communist dictatorship; the quieter corruption of mature totalitarianism. In the early 1990s it was a regular occurrence for a prominent East German politician, academic, journalist or priest to be identified through the Stasi files as an IM and to disappear from public life as a result. IM is the black spot.

But first they have to be identified. For the secret police assigned aliases to their informers as well as to those they were pursuing. In fact, most informers did it themselves, for one of the rituals of initiation as a regular IM was to choose your own secret name. It emerged after unification that one Lutz Bertram, a well-known blind East German disc jockey, had informed for the Stasi as IM 'Romeo'. If he and I had met, I suppose Romeo could have informed on Romeo.

My opening report summarizes the information gathered by

IM 'Smith', IM 'Schuldt' and, especially, by IM 'Michaela' and her husband, KP (Contact Person) 'Georg', previously married to Alice, known as 'Red Lizzy'. Lieutenant Wendt notes that 'Red Lizzy' had herself earlier been married to Kim Philby – Britain's most famous Soviet spy.

He finds that 'G. works purposefully and with scholarly thoroughness' but displays 'a bourgeois-liberal attitude and no commitment to the working class'. 'Outwardly G. makes a pretty casual impression and overall seems "a typical British intellectual".' (This strange compliment is from IM 'Smith'.) However, I have sought contact with people who could be of interest for intelligence purposes and given contradictory accounts of what I am doing. On my journeys to Poland I almost certainly 'maintain connections with anti-socialist forces'. So they need to find out more, with a view to possible prosecution under Article 97 of the Criminal Code. Article 97 says that anyone who collects or passes on 'information or objects which are to be kept secret' to a foreign power, or a secret service, or other unspecified 'foreign organizations', is to be punished with a jail sentence of 'not less than five years'. 'In especially serious cases a lifelong jail sentence or a death sentence may be passed.'

The 'plan of action' which follows has four parts. First, there is the deployment of IMs, starting with 'Smith': 'Taking account of the subjective and objective possibilities of the IM, conditions for the resumption of the lost contact with Garton Ash are to be created.' A written proposal is to be produced by 15 April 1981. 'Responsible: Lieutenant Wendt.' 'Schuldt' and 'Michaela' are also to be reactivated: written proposal from Lieutenant Wendt by 1 May. Furthermore, 'an IM of the HVA I – adviser of G. at the H[umboldt] U[niversity] B[erlin]' is to be brought in to 'the operational treatment'.

The HVA was the foreign intelligence service of East Germany. Its full name was *Hauptverwaltung Aufklärung* which, since the more usual meaning of *Aufklärung* is Enlightenment, could be translated as the Department of Enlightenment. Headed by Markus 'Mischa' Wolf, it was famously fictionalized as 'the Abteilung' in John le Carré's *The Spy Who Came In From The Cold*. Its first department, HVA I, was responsible for spying on the West German government in Bonn.

Next the plan turns to 'operational observation and investigation'. The measures to be taken include further investigation of Mr and Mrs Kreisel, the couple from whom the Humboldt University had rented my room with a view. A third category, 'further measures', gives instructions for a 'search' by Main Department VI, responsible for controlling cross-frontier traffic, and for department M to begin a 'post-control'. 'West Berlin address of G.', it says, but this presumably refers to letters coming from my West Berlin flat, since only in exceptional circumstances was the Stasi able to open someone's post in the West. And then, again for Lieutenant Wendt, the task of compiling a report on whether to turn this OPK investigation into a full-blown Operational Case, or OV. OV was the top category of operation, covering known opponents and critics of the regime. My friend Werner Krätschell, for example, appears here as OV 'Beech-tree'.

Finally there is 'cooperation with other service units'. Here coordination is proposed with department XX/4 (charged with infiltrating the churches) in respect of my contact with the Reverend Beech-tree. Enquiries are to be made 'to the Soviet security organs about possible current interest of the British Secret Service in information on the Philby case'. 'Concrete coordination' is to be pursued with AG4 to see if it would be possible to 'attach' informers to me during my visits to Poland. AG4 was a Stasi working group established to follow the alarming development of the Solidarity revolution in Poland. Responsible: Major Risse.

Signed by Lieutenant Wendt and counter-signed by Lieutenant-Colonel Kaulfuss, head of II/9, the department covering all West European intelligence services.

So that was their 'plan of action', then. My plan of action, now, is to investigate their investigation of me. I shall pursue their enquiry through this file, try to track down both the informers and the officers on my case, consult other files, compare the Stasi record with my own memories, with the diary and notes I kept at the time, and with the political history I have since written about this period. And I shall see what I find.

The cumbersomely named Federal Authority for the Records of the State Security Service of the former German Democratic Republic is usually called the Gauck Authority for short, after Joachim Gauck, the forceful and eloquent East German priest who heads it. My file comes from the Gauck Authority's main archive in Berlin, which is, in fact, the former central archive of the Ministry for State Security. The Ministry had a huge complex of office buildings, occupying a block-and-a-half on the Normannenstrasse in the east end of East Berlin. The Minister's offices and private apartment have been kept much as he left them: his desk with the many telephones (secret, top secret, ultra top secret), his tidy little bedroom, a tray of clay models presented to him by children at the 'Richard Sorge' kindergarten. There's a clay banana, a gnome, a little dog marked 'Jeanine', a lemon from 'Christin'.

Most of the other buildings have been given over to new purposes. All the external windows were once specially sealed so that no secret papers could be smuggled out by a double agent, or simply blown away by some careless draught. Now the windows are unsealed. Where the Kaulfusses and Wendts plied their dreary trade, there are now ordinary offices, a supermarket, Ritters Sport-sauna and a labour exchange. But the archive is working still.

In the catalogue room, middle-aged women in bright pink jumpers and nylon trousers patter around on plastic sandals between the huge card-index machines. I say machines because they are motorized. The actual card-index boxes are suspended from axles, like the cars on a fairground big wheel. Press the button for 'K' and the big wheel grinds round until the 'K' cards are uppermost. The F16 index – the abbreviation refers to the type of card – contains real names, but they are ordered according to the Stasi's own phonetic alphabet, so that, for example, Mueller, Muller, Möller and Müller are all filed together. (If you pick up names by bugging or phone-tapping, you don't know exactly how they are spelt.) From here, the ladies in pink patter off to check the F22 index – arranged by case numbers – and sometimes also the officers' individual case books, before finding the actual files in purpose-made stacks on one of the building's seven specially reinforced floors. Pitter-patter, pitter-pat go the plastic sandals, as the archive churns out its daily quota of poisoned madeleines.

Down the corridor, they show you the 'tradition room'. Medals, busts of Lenin, certificates of merit, banners celebrating the work of 'Chekists', the Soviet term for secret police officers: 'He alone may be a Chekist who has a cool head, a warm heart and clean hands (F. Dzerzhinsky).' On the table there are what look like jam jars. Each one is carefully labelled and contains a small piece of dirty yellow velveteen. These are samples of personal smell, taken so that, if need be, sniffer dogs could be given the scent. According to the Stasi dictionary, the correct term for them is 'smell conserve'. I stand there, stricken with a wild surmise. Perhaps somewhere in this vast building my own past smell is still conserved like jam?

Nearby there is what they call the 'copper cauldron', a

cavernous, metal-lined room in which the Ministry had planned to put a vast new computer system, containing all the information on everybody. The metal was to insulate it from outside electronic interference. Instead, the copper cauldron now contains hundreds of sacks stuffed with paper: documents torn up in the weeks between the beginning of mass protest in the autumn of 1989 and the storming of the Ministry in early 1990. On the plausible assumption that the Stasi would have started by destroying the most important and sensitive papers, the Gauck Authority is now trying to reconstruct them, shred by shred.

It's a weird place, this Gauck Authority: a ministry of truth occupying the former ministry of fear. Back at the administrative headquarters in central Berlin, there are long echoing corridors with new West German lights and plastic flooring, but still a faint residue of that unmistakable East Berlin smell. Lugubrious, beer-bellied porters at the door, elaborate visitors' passes, regulations, small-print, forms in triplicate, expenses – all the ponderous apparatus of German bureaucracy. And the habits of a bloated welfare state. As in so many German institutions, every second employee seems to be out to lunch, or on holiday, or 'at the doctor's'. The time-honoured recognition signal of the German office-worker, '*Mahlzeit!*' (Have a good meal!), echoes down the corridors. 'May I use your shredder?' one secretary asks another. For a moment you imagine a successor ministry piecing together these shredded documents, in a kind of infinite regression.

Meanwhile, every page of every document you get to see has been *re-numbered* by the Authority's archivists, with a neat rubber stamp over the Stasi's own careful handwritten pagination. It's like a parody of German thoroughness. One extreme follows the other. Probably no dictatorship in modern history has had such an extensive and fanatically thorough secret police as East Germany did. No democracy in modern history has done more to expose the legacy of the preceding dictatorship than the new Germany has.

A special law, passed by the parliament of united Germany in 1991, carefully regulates how the files can be used. Frau Schulz has read my file before me because she is supposed, in scrupulous bureaucratic implementation of that law, to photocopy the pages on which the names of Stasi victims or innocent third parties appear, to black out those names on the copies and then to copy the pages again, just to make quite sure the name cannot be deciphered using a strong light. She is also meant to cover up any passage containing personal information about other people which is not directly related to the enquiry. But what is not relevant to understanding a secret police which worked precisely by collecting and exploiting the most intimate details of private life?

The effect of reading a file can be terrible. I think of the now famous case of Vera Wollenberger, a political activist from Werner Krätschell's parish in Pankow, who discovered from reading her file that her husband, Knud, had been informing on her ever since they met. They would go for a walk with the children on Sunday, and on Monday Knud would be off pouring it all out to his Stasi case officer. She thought she had been married to Knud; she found she had been married to IM 'Donald'. (Vera refers to him in a memoir as 'Knud-Donald' or 'Donald-Knud'. They are now divorced.) Or the writer Hans Joachim Schädlich, who found that his elder brother had been informing on him. And they only discovered from the files. Had the files not been opened, they might still be brother and brother, man and wife – their love enduring, a fortress sure upon the rock of lies.

There are also lighter side-effects. After the law came into force, students at the Humboldt University in East Berlin would go around boasting to their girlfriends: 'Of course I've put in to see my file. I dread to think what I'll find there, but I simply have to know.' Luscious Sabine would be really impressed. Then came the dreadful letter from the Authority: so far as we can establish, you have no file. Humiliation. Sabine turned to someone else, who had.

When I tell people about my file, they say strange things like, 'how lucky!' or 'what a privilege!' If they themselves had anything to do with Eastern Europe, they say, 'yes, I must apply to see my file', or, 'it seems that mine was destroyed', or, 'Gauck tells me mine is probably in Moscow'. No one ever says 'I'm sure they didn't have one on me.' One could almost describe the syndrome in Freudian terms: file-envy.

Actually, mine is very modest compared to many. What is my single binder, against the writer Jürgen Fuchs's thirty? What are my 325 pages against the 40,000 they devoted to the dissident singer Wolf Biermann? Yet small keys can open large doors, and this is a way into much bigger rooms. Wherever there has been a secret police, not just in Germany, people often protest that such files are wholly unreliable, full of distortions and fabrications. How better to start testing that claim than by seeing what they had on me? After all, I should know what I was really up to. And what did my officers and informers think they were doing? Can the files, and the men and women behind them, tell us anything more about communism, the Cold War and the sense or nonsense of spying? This systematic opening of secret police records, to every citizen who is in them and still wants to know, is without precedent. There has been nothing like it, anywhere, ever. Was it right? What has it done to those involved? The experience may even teach us something about history and memory, about ourselves, about human nature. So if the form of this book seems self-indulgent, the purpose is not. I am but a window, a sample, a means to an end, the object in this experiment.

To do this, I must explore not just a file but a life: The life of the person I was then. This, in case you were wondering, is not the same thing as 'my life'. What we call 'my life' is but a constantly rewritten version of our own past. 'My life' is the mental autobiography with which and by which we all live. What really happened is quite another matter.

By searching for a lost self I am also searching for a lost time. And for answers to the question: how did the one shape the other? Historical time and personal time, the public and the private, great events and our own lives. Writing about the large areas of human experience ignored by conventional political history, the historian Keith Thomas quotes Samuel Johnson:

> How small, of all that human hearts endure
> That part which laws or kings can cause or cure.

But looking back I see how much the experience of my own heart, at least, was caused by our modern 'laws and kings': by the different regimes of East and West, and the conflict between them. Perhaps, after all, Johnson was expressing not a universal but a purely local truth. Happy the country where that was ever true.

II

I SET OFF FOR BERLIN on my twenty-third birthday, 12 July 1978, driving my new, dark-blue Alfa-Romeo up the motorway to the Harwich ferry terminal. From the Hoek van Holland, I raced down the autobahn to the Helmstedt frontier crossing at the 'iron curtain' between West and East Germany, then nervously observed the speed limit on the designated transit route across East Germany to West Berlin. I lived in West Berlin for a year-and-a-half, before driving through Checkpoint Charlie on 7 January 1980, to that room in East Berlin. My original purpose was to write an Oxford doctoral thesis about Berlin under Hitler.

For this period, from July 1978 to January 1980, the Chronology I recently compiled for my history of Germany and the divided continent lists major political events from 'Summit of world's leading industrial countries (G7) in Bonn' to 'President Carter announces sanctions against Soviet Union, interrupts ratification of SALT II treaty and threatens boycott of Moscow Olympics'. In between it notes the election of Karol Wojtyła as Pope John Paul II and his first Papal visit to Poland, the first direct elections to the European Parliament, Nato's 'twin-track' decision (to deploy new nuclear missiles in Europe if the Soviet Union would not negotiate a reduction in theirs) and the Soviet invasion of Afghanistan in December 1979. We see now that this was the build-up to the last great confrontation of the Cold War: Reagan versus Brezhnev, American cruise missiles against Soviet SS20s, the Polish revolution in the East and the peace movement in the West.

My own diary has a quite different chronology. Instead of the G7 summit, I note a long conversation with the poet James Fenton about German literature, Macaulay and the (remote) possibility of journalism being an art form. Instead of the crucial January 1979 Guadeloupe summit, which led to the Nato twin-track decision, I have lunch with Jay Reddaway, a friend from undergraduate days, at the Café Moskau in East Berlin and then an evening in West Berlin which apparently proceeds via drinks at 'Bilitis' to dinner at 'Foofie's' (can this be real?) and then more drink at 'Ax Bax'. The Pope in Poland does feature, but the first direct elections to the European Parliament find me having breakfast at the Café Einstein, visiting an art gallery and failing to complete an article for the *Spectator*.

Where the historical chronology dourly records 'Gromyko in Bonn', I am in Franconia, drinking too much smoked beer and visiting the scene of Hitler's Nuremberg rally. The Soviet invasion of Afghanistan finds me on the night-train to visit Albert Speer at his gingerbread house in Heidelberg. While Jimmy Carter is threatening sanctions against the Soviet Union, I am occupied with preparations for a party. So much for living 'in the heat of the Cold War' – to use the deliberately mixed metaphor of my friend Mark Wood, the Reuters correspondent in East Berlin.

For this year-and-a-half, the Stasi's intelligence is fragmentary. There is the observation report on my East Berlin evening with 'Beret'. In a summary report from department XX/4 (churches), they have correctly identified 'Beret', as well as listing two other West Berlin contacts, Ingrid [surname blacked out by Frau Schulz] and Heinrich [surname also obscured], together with my West Berlin telephone number. They also record that I was born in a place called Winbredow (that is, Wimbledon), describe my Oxford college as 'St. ansowts' (St Antony's) and give a date that is wrong by three months for a journey to Poland. They indicate that I am working, together with the English citizen Morris [surname blacked out], on the conflict between the churches and the regime in Nazi Germany. However, 'it has been established that G. has extensive knowledge of cultural monuments and places, cultural [sic] and cultural personalities of the GDR and especially of the Bauhaus problematic. In June 1979 G. first identified himself as a so-called freelance contributor to the English weekly "Spekta", which wished to write a report on the anti-fascist resistance struggle.' The man from *Spekta*.

This information derives mainly from department XX/4's own enquiry into the Reverend Beech-tree and from a four-page report by Lieutenant Küntzel of the Erfurt office, following a meeting with Contact Person 'Georg' and IMV 'Michaela'. The V after the IM indicates that 'Michaela' belonged to the Stasi's highest class of informer, those deployed in direct contact with the enemy. Lieutenant Küntzel reports that on 30 June 1979 Dr Georg [surname blacked out], living in Schloss [name blacked out] in Weimar, was visited by an unknown person with an English or American accent who introduced himself as Tim Gartow-Ash, a freelance contributor to the English weekly 'Spacktator'.

This blacking-out is, as you can see, often ineffectual, for there cannot have been many Dr Georg [somebodies] living in a Schloss in Weimar. On the other hand, the law on the Stasi files grants the right to anonymity only to innocent third parties or victims, not to collaborators. A glance at my diary establishes the identity of Dr Georg, as well as the fact that the Stasi have again got the date wrong.

Dr Georg was one of those older Jewish communists who were among the most interesting people to talk to in East Germany, indeed throughout communist-ruled Europe. I probably knew at the time I visited him that he had been the editor of an East Berlin daily paper and head of an officially tolerated satirical cabaret, and perhaps I also knew that he had spent the Nazi period in England, where he worked for Reuters. It was only later I learned that in England he had met and subsequently married Alice 'Litzi' Kohlman, the warm and energetic Austro-Hungarian-Jewish woman who had been Kim Philby's first wife and, by some accounts, instrumental in leading the young Englishman on to work as a Soviet spy. Only from this Stasi report do I discover that Dr Georg had himself worked for Soviet intelligence during his time at Reuters.

With that background, it is hardly surprising that he was suspicious of the story with which I came to him. According to Lieutenant Küntzel, Dr Georg rapidly established that I did not actually know the person – Sanda [name blacked out] – who I claimed had suggested that I should visit him. When I asked how he came to speak such good English, he told me that he had spent many years in England, where he worked for Reuters: 'At this G. pretended to be interested and asked if one [name blacked out] had at that time been Director of "Reuter". When this question was answered affirmatively, G. broke out in expressions of delight: "Imagine, what a coincidence, Chancellor's son is now my superior (*Vorgesetzter*)." The whole outburst was well feigned, but [Dr Georg] could detect that G. knew about his work for "Reuter". Having become suspicious and being strengthened in the feeling that the attempt to make contact with him had another character than that claimed, [Dr. Georg] became reticent towards G., without, however, appearing impolite.'

This passage illustrates in miniature how small distortions creep in to Stasi records. For example, I would certainly never have referred to the genial Alexander Chancellor, then Editor of the *Spectator*, as my *Vorgesetzter*, a word with clear implications of hierarchical command. This must be Dr Georg's word or – more likely – Lieutenant Küntzel's, for the Lieutenant lived in a world where everyone had a *Vorgesetzter*. Yet there it is: attributed to me as part of a direct quotation. Now suppose for a moment that the content of this passage were altogether more serious and compromising, suppose that the interpretation of the whole passage hinged – as it sometimes can – on the one word; suppose I had subsequently become a prominent East German politician; and suppose that I woke up one morning to find the passage quoted against me as a headline in a West German tabloid: quote unquote. Calls for resignation follow. Who would believe me when I protested: 'No, I didn't say that! Well, not *exactly*. And anyway, they've got the date wrong. And the title of the *Spectator*. And the spelling of my name . . .'

Yet despite the small distortions and inaccuracies, this account basically rings true. Whether or not I actually knew beforehand about Dr Georg's connection with Reuters – of which Alexander Chancellor's father, Christopher Chancellor, had been General Manager – I can just hear myself overplaying my delight at this rather unremarkable coincidence, in the hope of keeping a rather sticky conversation going and getting Dr Georg to talk more freely.

'At this time the wife (IMV 'Michaela') of [Dr Georg], who had been in the kitchen, entered the living room', the report continues. 'She was introduced by her husband with the words: "My wife, director of the Weimar Art Galleries." The IMV thought the visit was to her husband . . . so she was all the more surprised that G. immediately brought the subject round to the exhibition on the Bauhaus organized by the Art Galleries. He explained that he had seen the exhibition and was fascinated by it. However he could not understand why the Art Galleries had not issued a catalogue. The way the question was posed suggested that he would have liked to have heard from the IMV that this was impossible for reasons of cultural policy. The IMV did not go into that, but explained it by the paper shortage . . .

'Angered by the rudeness of G., who now only let [Dr. Georg] be a silent listener to the conversation, no longer mentioning the original subject, [Dr Georg] took his leave of G. on the pretence of having to run an errand in town. At this point the conversation had lasted some 40 minutes. Now G. explained to the IMV that he was working on an article about the development of the artistic and cultural life of the GDR and was therefore interested in the IMV's comments. He posed such questions as:

– why was there only now a Bauhaus exhibition organized in the GDR (Weimar)?
– what is the attitude of the GDR to the Bauhaus?
– what reception did the exhibition have nationally?
– what reception did the exhibition have internationally?

In the conversation it became clear that G. has a good knowledge of the artistic scene, especially in the field of the Bauhaus.'

At the end of the visit I apparently wrote my name on a piece of paper – 'for unknown reasons he did not wish to give the full address' – and expressed interest in further conversations. 'The conversation with the IMV lasted 20 minutes, so that G. spent in all about one hour in the apartment.'

Lieutenant Küntzel finds all this of 'operational relevance' for a number of reasons. He notes that Dr Georg might be of interest to 'enemy agencies' because of his earlier connection with Kim Philby but also because in East Germany he is disgruntled with current cultural policy and may have sympathy for 'dissidents' (Küntzel's quotation marks). Those enemy agencies, speculates the Lieutenant, might be interested in the possibility of 'building up a dissident' (his quotation marks again). So Dr Georg is at once source and suspect.

Meanwhile, I am highly suspect because, in the Lieutenant's

analysis, I used not just one but three 'legends' to describe what I was really about: friend of a friend, journalist, student of East German cultural life. 'Legend' is the Stasi term for cover story. It is generally used for the stories developed for their own full-time agents and part-time informers, but here is applied by extension to me.

Measures to be taken include telling 'Michaela' and 'Georg' what to do if I contacted them again and informing counter-intelligence department II/13, which was responsible for watching Western journalists.

Some of the small details are wrong. The interpretation is paranoid. Yet overall, the Stasi lives up to its reputation for being everywhere and watching everyone. On account of just one incautious conversation, and a couple of more or less innocent contacts, I have already been entered in to the central files as a suspect. By the time I am preparing to cross to East Berlin, after eighteen months in the West, they have pulled together in a summary report their information on my contacts, my West Berlin address and telephone number, my car, my hair, my height (corrected on the file copy to 1.80 metres, from 'Michaela's' estimate of between 1.65 and 1.70 metres), even the fact that I appear to be a non-smoker.

However, it is also striking what they have missed. For example, there is no indication of broadcasts I had done for the BBC in Berlin, or the articles I had already written for the *Spectator* about East Germany, including a tribute to East Germany's most prominent dissident, Robert Havemann. 'Edward Marston', the pseudonym under which I wrote, seems to have been an effective disguise. Nor is there any record of the Christmas I spent with friends near Dresden, and many other visits.

Not surprisingly, they have little on my life in West Berlin.

Yet even the partly blacked-out names, addresses and telephone numbers unlock memory's doors and send me back to my diary.

WHEN I ARRIVED in Berlin, fresh from England, I drove to the flat of an old lady called Ursula von Krosigk, to whom I had been introduced by the publisher Graham Greene, a nephew of the novelist. Graham's father, Hugh Greene, had known her when he was *Daily Telegraph* correspondent in Berlin during the 1930s, before being expelled by the Nazis. Ursula was white-haired, bolt upright, never married, a Prussian noblewoman through and through, but warm-hearted, spontaneous and unconventional. Her characteristic, defiant toss of the head somehow still recalled the naughty schoolgirl playing truant from her grim boarding school in Potsdam fifty years before. She had lived in Berlin most of her life, and once described to me how the smartly-dressed crowd at the premiere of Brecht's *Threepenny Opera* swept out of the brightly-lit theatre past a row of real-life beggars – unemployed cripples, war-wounded – in the shadows along the Schiffbauerdamm. Many of her friends had been involved in the resistance to Hitler, but her uncle, Lutz Schwerin von Krosigk, had been Hitler's finance minister. She remembered driving out with him to his country estate on the morning after *Kristallnacht*, through streets littered with the broken glass and debris from plundered Jewish shops: 'No one said a word.'

Ursula lived on the fourth floor of a nineteenth-century apartment block, at a quiet corner of the Pariserstrasse in prosperous Wilmersdorf. From the window, you looked past trees to a red-brick Wilhelmine church. Downstairs there was a rather grand marble staircase and a huge double-door made of wrought metal and glass. To get in or out at night, after the porter had locked up, each tenant had an ingenious iron key which you put in one side of the keyhole and pulled out the other. I remember my sense of excitement on that first warm summer's evening as the heavy door closed behind me and I set out to explore the fabled city.

Indoors, the flat was full of once-fine pieces of furniture and overflowing with books. I slept in a sleeping-bag on the draw-ing-room floor, next to a dusty old sofa propped up by a pre-war Baedeker of Dresden; and as I drifted off to sleep I reflected that propping up a sofa was about all that a pre-war Baedeker of Dresden would be good for. I was on the floor because Ursula already had a lodger in her spare room. This was James Fenton, who had come to Berlin as a special correspondent for the *Guardian*, after writing about literature, Indo-China and West-minster politics for the *New Statesman*.

James and I were soon spending a good deal of time together. My diary notes long evenings, over many cold beers and chasers, at our local trendy bistro, curiously called Bistroquet; or at the corner pub across the square, the far-from trendy Kuchel-Eck, with its doilies, fruit machines and loudspeakers constantly playing 'By the Rivers of Babylon'; or at the Presse-Bar, which we liked because no-one from the press ever went near it; or Zwiebelfisch and Ax Bax, favoured haunts of now paunchy sur-vivors of the 1968 events; or the bourgeois Café Möhring; or the Dicke Wirtin (The Fat Landlady) where, in the early hours, a desperate Algerian at the next table burned his residence permit and a drunken man in a black-leather jacket then pulled a gun on him.

'Watch out, he's got a gun!' said James.

'That's impossible,' said the German girl with us, who worked for the British Military Government in the still-occupied city, 'private handguns are forbidden in Berlin.' But the gun was real. Pale, intense, shabbily dressed, his body slightly bowed beneath his large, tonsured head, James was like a dissident monk. His initial knowledge of Germany, and German, was not large. In fact, the local German correspondents at first thought he must be a spy since, they rather strangely reasoned, no journalist could know so little about the country to which he was despatched. This did not last long, however, since he had a very sharp eye, an equally sharp mind and the crusading journalist's passionate tenacity in pursuing a story – especially where it involved wrongdoing by the rich, the powerful or the sanctimonious.

For various reasons, some of which I perhaps hardly guessed at, this was not a happy time for him, but for me he was an enchanting companion. What set him apart was the poet's verbal wit and fantasy, unexpectedly, whimsically and sometimes crazily taking flight from the shared ground of experiences that were already interesting enough. I learned much from him about the craft of writing, and we became close friends.

In the autumn, Ursula gave up her flat and went to live in Munich. We decamped a few blocks down the Pariserstrasse, to the pleasingly tawdry Pension Pariser-Eck: all orange lamps and noises through thin walls, very Graham Greene. As autumn turned to a bitterly cold Berlin winter, and the east wind seemed to whistle down the Kurfürstendamm straight from Siberia, we moved, with impeccably bad timing, into a small flat heated by an old-fashioned, tile-clad corner stove. The stove needed constant feeding with coke briquettes, which we had to carry up from the cellar. I briefly fled this hardship in the West for luxury in the East, celebrating a traditional German Christmas Eve with my new-found friends the Krügers, an upper-middle class family who lived an extraordinary life of 'inner emigration' behind the high garden walls of their *fin-de-siècle* family villa in

Radebeul, near Dresden. On the way, my car, unaccustomed to northern snows, refused to start again on the East German side of Checkpoint Charlie. The guards gave me a jovial push-start into the East.

When visitors came from Britain, James and I would take them to the Paris Bar in the Kantstrasse, to Exil, a restaurant in Kreuzberg run by 'exiles' from Vienna, to Romy Haag's raucous transvestite cabaret and then on to another bar or two. Berlin had to live up to the Isherwood myth. I assigned the part of Sally Bowles to a new friend of mine called Irene Dische, an attractive American girl of German-Jewish origin, who had come to Berlin to be a writer. Talking to Irene now, I see that of course she had us down as Auden and Isherwood – or was it Spender?

In real life, our West Berlin experience was shaped less by the shades of Isherwood than by those of the '68 revolt, of which West Berlin had been a centre, alongside Paris, Amsterdam, Frankfurt and Berkeley. Ten years on, there was no longer the special shop on the Uhlandstrasse where you could buy everything you needed for a demo – red flag, placard, gas mask, suitable boots. But the walls of the Free University were still covered with political graffiti and at least half our friends belonged – like Claudia – to the 1968 generation. You could recognize the '68er at once: the jeans and open shirt; the inevitable cigarette or joint; the instant *Du* rather than the more usual and formal *Sie*; the distinctive vocabulary, with lots of socio-psycho neologisms about relationships, 'structural violence' and so on. The apartment would have bare floorboards, white painted walls and a pine bookshelf with serial copies of the journal *Kursbuch* and the totemic books by Enzensberger, Bloch, Adorno and Marcuse.

Yet those who had marched together in '68 were walking in different directions now. A few had become terrorists in the

Red Army Faction (otherwise known as the Baader-Meinhof gang) or rival grouplets, planting bombs and assassinating prominent businessmen or senior officials. The West German state had responded with a heavy hand, banning even suspected 'enemies of the constitution' from state employment, which in Germany covered an extraordinarily wide range of jobs, from top civil servants to postmen and street cleaners: '*Berufsverbot*', the critics dubbed it. Soon after I arrived, there appeared a gloomy film called *Germany in Autumn*, full of mounted police and sinister, dark-suited establishment figures. Was Germany going bad again?

Some of these friends would tell us how there had been a moment back in the late 1960s or early 1970s when they, too, might have become terrorists. But instead they had – despite *Berufsverbot* – become teachers, or social workers, or academics. Or they had gone back to poetry and painting, or on to publishing and journalism, or got into other isms: environmentalism, feminism, structuralism. Claudia was a schoolteacher, Paul an eternal student and part-time art dealer, Peter an artist, Yvonne a psychologist and translator, Elmar a political scientist. Friedrich was a freelance journalist, now embarked on a crusading investigation of the way in which the West German courts had failed to pursue Nazi crimes – and especially the crimes of German lawyers and judges themselves. Here was a particular interest of the German '68ers: exposing the sins of the fathers.

Early in 1979, I moved into what was called a *Wohngemeinschaft* – the '68ers term for a communal flat – in the Traunsteinerstrasse in Schöneberg. My flatmates, or fellow communards, were a nice, mildly left-wing American academic called Hugh and a man called Bernd. Bernd's father had worked for the Nazis as an aircraft engineer, and then been carried off by the Americans to work for them. In the wake of 1968, Bernd had become not just a leftist but a member of the Socialist Unity

Party of Westberlin, a puppet-sister of East Germany's ruling communist party. He wanted, as he tells me now, to join something that was 'serious', by which he meant, connected to real power. At that time it still looked as if Soviet power was growing, while, after Vietnam, that of the United States seemed to be fading. Helped by his Party card, Bernd had got a job with an East-West trading company which was, though I did not know it at the time, a direct subsidiary of an East German enterprise with close connections to the Stasi.

Bernd was a heavily built, irascible man, with a brow that creased into thick worry-lines. His touch could not be described as light. Nazism and Marxism furnished his spontaneous terms of reference and abuse. My diary records that when I overstayed my allotted time in the bathroom one morning, so that his careful daily routine was disrupted, he beat on the door with his fists and shouted 'ruling class!' When Heiner, the main tenant, threatened to sue him for having his children in the flat, Bernd retorted: 'You Nazi pig. You're like the concentration camp guard who murders people during the day and then plays the piano and drinks his wine in the evening . . .'

In fact I owed my place in the commune to this titanic quarrel between the two of them, which had resulted in Heiner moving out. Before he left me his two beautiful, airy, high-ceilinged rooms, with an arrangement of empty picture-frames on the white-painted walls, he sat me down for a chat. By candlelight, and through clouds of cigarette-smoke, I found myself launched into a two-and-a-half hour psychoanalytic session, which mainly consisted of Heiner talking about himself. I record one characteristic passage describing how he had seen himself at the age of fourteen: 'At that time I started from the assumption that I was strongly ego-positive, heterosexual, but perhaps with anal aspects.' All this just to hand over the keys.

When he had gone, I noted the contrast with Jay, the British public-school-and-Oxford friend who had just visited me: 'from the reserved, oblique, ironical, snobbish, inhibited, emotionally-tangled Englishman to the open, direct, earnest, left-wing, jargon-ridden, liberated, emotionally-tangled German.' A few days later, the telephone rang. I picked up.

'Hello, is Heiner there?' asked the anonymous caller.

'No.'

'Well, are you gay?' – he used the German word *schwul*.

'No', I said, and put the phone down. Seconds later, it rang again.

'Hello,' said the same voice, 'are you an Englishman?'

'Yes.'

'Well, what I meant was: do you sleep with men?'

'No!'

Heiner, I now discover from Bernd, had decided a couple of years earlier that he was homosexual and at that time was exploring the matter, programmatically. But I don't think that he was necessarily making a pass at me. He may just have thought he was making me feel at home.

Bernd now tells me that Heiner recently died of Aids.

I HAD MIXED FEELINGS about the '68ers. They were interesting just because they were so unlike most people I had known. I could understand and sympathize with some of their political projects: for example, Friedrich's campaign to expose the failure to do justice to the victims of Nazi injustice. However, they seemed to me often hysterical, self-obsessed and self-indulgent. I tired of their moaning about problems that struck me either as self-created or as minor compared to those in the East. Heiner told me that President Carter's visit to West Berlin was just like a visit by Brezhnev to an East European satrap, yet he appeared totally indifferent to what was happening in the professedly socialist state of East Germany, just a few miles away, behind the Wall. For them, the Wall which encircled West Berlin seemed to be nothing but a huge mirror in which they could contemplate themselves and their own 'relationships'. 'The paper narcissi', says my diary.

Yet if the '68ers were exotic to me, this heavy-shoed, tweed-jacketed young Englishman must have been a strange apparition to them. Looking back, he now seems pretty odd to me. People may envy the possessor of a file, but being carried off by your poisoned madeleine is not always a comfortable experience. In his novel *Ferdydurke*, the Polish writer Witold Gombrowicz imagines waking up one day to find himself sixteen again. He hears his 'long-buried, squawky little rooster voice', sees his 'ungrown nose on an unformed face' and senses that his ill-mixed limbs are laughing at each other: the nose mocking the leg, the leg sneering at the ear. Time-travel with a file can be rather like that: a bad trip.

What the Stasi's Lieutenant Küntzel called my 'legends' were in truth less cover stories than different strands of an unformed life. Like the confused, ambitious twenty-three-year-old graduate students who now come to my rooms in Oxford to ask me for life-advice, I wanted to do everything at once: to write a doctoral thesis about Berlin in the Third Reich, and a book about East Germany, and an essay about the Bauhaus, and brilliant reports for the *Spectator*, and probably to be George Orwell, Foreign Secretary and war hero too. Cover stories that I told myself.

The diary reminds me of all the fumblings, the clumsiness, the pretentiousness and snobbery – and the insouciance with which I barged into other people's lives. Embarrassment apart, there is the sheer difficulty of reconstructing how you really thought and felt. How much easier to do it to other people! At times, this past self is such a stranger to me that where I have written 'I' in these last pages I almost feel it should be 'he'.

Personal memory is such a slippery customer. Nietzsche catches it brilliantly in one of his epigrams: ' "I did that", says my memory. "I can't have done that", says my pride and remains adamant. In the end – memory gives way.' The temptation is always to pick and choose your past, just as it is for nations: to remember Shakespeare and Churchill but forget Northern Ireland. But we must take it all or leave it all, and I must say 'I'.

FOR ALL THE DISTRACTIONS, my diary still records me spending long, weary hours working through Gestapo files in the sinister-sounding Secret Prussian State Archive, and the records of the Nazis' so-called People's Court in the Berlin Document Center. The People's Court papers were piled on metal shelves, dusty and uncatalogued, while the American director of the Document Center, then still an institution of the American military government, went off to play golf.

I was appalled at the number of prosecutions that began with a denunciation, not by paid Gestapo informers but by ordinary people: a barber, denounced by a customer; a chemist, denounced by his shop assistant; a housekeeper, denounced by her employers; even someone informing on his own brother and a wife accusing her husband. These are all real cases – taken from People's Court judgments that I xeroxed at the time. Many of these trials led to a death sentence.

At the end of the day I would step out into the sunlit streets of leafy Grunewald, sickened by this seemingly endless record of human baseness and cruelty. Often I felt as if I had blood on my own hands. I would go for a swim, to wash the blood off. Then I would have a drink at a café and look at the old women gossiping at the next table. What did you do in the war, granny?

I did not confine myself to the archives. I also talked to the veterans and survivors. There was Albert Speer in Heidelberg, with his well-polished tale of the unpolitical technocrat. There were casual acquaintances, each with an extraordinary personal history: a motor mechanic, for example, whose parents died while he was still a baby on the desperate flight west before the advancing Red Army, so that he knew neither his birthplace, nor his birthday, nor his real name. All that he knew is that he came from somewhere in the Memelland, a once-German territory in what is now Lithuania. Then there were the grand old men of the German resistance to Hitler who met again every year, on the anniversary of the 20 July 1944 bomb plot, in the courtyard of the former Wehrmacht headquarters where the leader of the plot, Count Stauffenberg, had stood before the firing squad.

Just before he died, Stauffenberg cried out in defiance *'Es lebe das heilige Deutschland!'* – 'Long live sacred Germany!' Or was it *'Es lebe das geheime Deutschland!'* – 'Long live secret Germany!' – a reference both to the resistance conspiracy and to the semi-mystical ideas of the poet Stefan George? Stauffenberg's last words are still disputed. Amidst the ghosts of secret Germany I was searching for the answer to a personal question. What is it that makes one person a resistance fighter and another the faithful servant of a dictatorship? This man a Stauffenberg, that a Speer. Today, after years of study, and after knowing personally many resisters and many servants of dictatorships, I am searching still.

Not just to a professional student of history but to any Englishman living in Germany at this time, and probably to most British newspaper readers, the past was still the most interesting thing about Germany – and 'the past' meant essentially the twelve years of Nazism. The great achievements of post-war reconstruction, the civilized democracy and exemplary social market economy presided over by Chancellor Helmut Schmidt: all were greatly admired, but boring. Even the far-left terrorist threat and the strong reaction of the West German state were given their special edge because of the fear, bequeathed by Hitler, that Germany could again be dangerous.

James was almost as fascinated as I was by the Nazi past, and we worked on several stories together. With Friedrich, our '68er journalist friend, we observed the trials of the Majdanek concentration camp guards in Düsseldorf. When an elderly Jewish woman testified that she had been forced as a prisoner to carry cannisters of the poison Zyklon B to the gas chambers, a German defence lawyer leapt to his feet demanding her instant arrest for aiding and abetting murder.

We also pursued the mysterious case of the then West German President's youthful membership of the Nazi party. A distinguished painter, Heinz Troekes, told us how the young Karl Carstens used proudly to wear his party badge at the artillery school where he was an instructor and Troekes a pupil. But President Carstens continued to win popularity by his knickerbockered rambling around the German countryside, and the story faded away. I was on the case as both fledgling historian and apprentice journalist, James as a fully-fledged journalist but also as a poet. Out of this experience he wrote one poem, 'A German Requiem', which captures better than anything else I know the elusive, haunted quality of German memory:

> How comforting it is, once or twice a year,
> To get together and forget the old times.

One evening, Friedrich rang to say that a neo-Nazi group called the Viking Youth would be out in force at the opening of a new pub called the Café Vaterland. He had seen some of them earlier at a discussion with schoolchildren about the American television series *Holocaust*, which was making a huge impact in Germany at this time. Their 'ideologist' had threatened that they would again erect concentration camps in Germany.

The Café Vaterland was on the ground floor of a nondescript modern block on the Tauentzienstrasse. The walls were decked with military bric-à-brac and a crude oil-painting showed Hitler sitting on the lavatory. When we arrived, the place was already half-filled with teenagers in leather jackets and boots. They ate bread smeared with dripping and greeted each other with a Peter Sellers version of the Nazi salute, stopping with a bent right arm, half way up. The rest of the pub was packed with journalists, observing these Viking Youths. At about midnight, since nothing seemed to be happening, we left and walked round the corner to where my car was parked in a dark street. Suddenly there were several black-jacketed figures running towards us. They carried beer bottles broken off at the base to give a jagged cutting edge.

At this point, my memory goes into slow motion. I see the thugs coming out of the darkness into the light of a street lamp. I see myself walking slowly – idiotically – round the car, to open the driver's door. James is on the pavement, vaguely brandishing a collapsible umbrella. Friedrich is running away diagonally across the street, towards a brightly lit multi-storey car-park on the other side. I don't remember at all the sensation of the bottle hitting me on the side of the head. Perhaps I lost consciousness for a few seconds, since the next thing I see is both James and Friedrich bending over me, as I begin to pick myself up off the dirty tarmac. I think I first realized what had happened from the horrified expressions on their faces, looming above me, garishly illuminated by the street. Then, to complete this B-movie sequence, I put my fingers to my neck, bring the hand down again and look at the blood.

One of the thugs had got me with a broken-off bottle just behind the ear. Dazed and bleeding, I was driven by a passing motorist to the nearest emergency department and sewn up by a very unsympathetic elderly nurse, while James and Friedrich loudly insisted on immediate access to a telephone. She said, 'Your friends there are worse than the Nazis.' Next day, a journalist from one of the German tabloids got annoyed with me because I had washed my bloodstained shirt, which he wanted to photograph. 'Where's the bloody shirt?' he demanded.

The East German communist party daily *Neues Deutschland* covered the story under the headline 'Playground for Fascists in Westberlin'. In line with the Marxist theory that fascism grows from capitalism, it reported that 'with the support of the beer company Dortmund Union-Schultheiss', the owners of the pub had:

> established a centre of Neo-nazism and Militarism in the middle of Westberlin. Members of the neo-nazi 'Viking Youth' felt encouraged to make their first terror actions against those with different political views. They threatened three journalists, among them two Englishmen who were working on a documentary on the Nazi Reich. They followed the journalists on to the street and beat them up. So far the state attorney has done nothing.

In fact, both the West Berlin authorities and the British military government took a close interest in the case. I was interviewed at length by the local security service. I was given a minute medical examination by one Dr Spengler, at a morgue. The Viking Youths were identified and arrested. We gave evidence at their trial in the forbidding court building of Moabit – Berlin's Old Bailey – and they were convicted.

James did not, however, share my special interest in East Germany, although my diary records one earnest conversation in which he appears to have said that the possibility of development within socialist societies was the most important political question for leftists like himself. What has happened to the Left since 1989 suggests that this was ultimately true. At the time though, it was a very hard truth for Western leftists to accept, especially for those who in 1968 had been confronted on the streets of West Berlin by horrible old women waving their umbrellas and screeching 'go over there!' (meaning, to the East).

The '68ers coped with this awkwardness in several awkward ways. Some now leaned over backwards – or was it forwards? – to see all the good and progressive elements in East Germany: social security, full employment, equal opportunities for women, kindergartens for all. As scholars or journalists they wrote idealized accounts of East Germany which added up to a quite comprehensive misunderstanding of their own country. Theirs was a revolt against the crude, Cold War anti-communism of their parents; it was less pro-communism than anti-anti-communism. It was also a hope against hope that the whole millennial project of socialism was not being discredited by the 'socialism' being practised in the East.

A few, like Bernd, became out-and-out defenders of the Eastern system, Wall and all. A few went further still. All the Stasi foreign intelligence officers I have now talked to, including Markus Wolf himself, tell me that the '68ers provided a rich field for the recruitment of agents. Numerically, of course, these agents were an insignificantly tiny part of that generation, but so were the terrorists. However, most of this political generation took none of these paths. Instead, they simply looked away. From West Germany, they looked and travelled west, south and north, but never east. Even in West Berlin they somehow managed this, although the East was all around them.

In James's case, I don't think ideological worries contributed much to his relative lack of interest in the East. When we talk about it again today, he reminds me that the *Guardian* had an Eastern Europe correspondent who protected her territory more jealously than Leonid Brezhnev. East Germany was part of her patch. If James tried to cross the Wall she would probably shoot to kill.

Born in 1949, James was an English '68er. I, six years younger, was not. The ideological evaluation in my Stasi opening report – 'bourgeois-liberal' – was just about right. I cared passionately for what I saw, with a rather simplistic romantic patriotism, as the British heritage of individual liberty. And I wanted this liberty for other people. My intellectual heroes were Macaulay, George Orwell and Isaiah Berlin. *'Ich bin ein Berliner'*, I used to say, meaning an Isaiah Berliner. With these personal politics, I was never likely to take a sympathetic view of East Germany. But liberal anti-communism was not the primary source of my fascination with the East. I was fascinated because here, in East Germany, people were actually *living* those endlessly difficult choices between collaboration with and resistance to a dictatorship. Here I could pursue the Stauffenberg/Speer question in, as it were, real time.

Here, too, I found that intimate proximity of high European culture and systematic inhumanity which George Steiner had identified in his *In Bluebeard's Castle*, a book that had made a great impression on me when I read it at the age of seventeen. In my diary, I called this phenomenon 'Goethe Oak', after the ancient oak tree on the Ettersberg, near Weimar, under which Goethe had supposedly written his sublime 'Wanderer's Night Song', but which was then enclosed in the grounds of the Buchenwald concentration camp. Goethe and Buchenwald, the highest and the lowest in human history, together in one place. A place called Weimar. A place called Germany. A place called Europe.

This fascination with dictatorship and resistance, with the extremes of good and evil, civilization and barbarism, also led me further into communist-ruled Europe. I travelled through Albania in the summer of 1978, on a 'Progressive Tour' with seven Marxist-Leninist teachers from Leeds, a Scottish engineer and a former imperial policeman called Mr Godsave. Over a cup of spirit-laced coffee known in communist Albania as a Lumumba – after the Congolese independence leader, Patrice Lumumba – Mr Godsave confided in me that he had now visited every communist country in the world. Why? 'Must get to know the enemy.'

The next summer, I drove through all six countries of what was then called Eastern Europe. In Poland, I discovered the spirit of resistance that I had long been seeking. Outwardly poor, dirty and neglected, though still with pockets of ancient beauty, the country was made magical by its people, now super-charged by the recent, incredible pilgrimage of a Polish Pope. In Kraków, over a beef dish presented as 'Nelson's bowels', giggling, indomitable Róża Woźniakowska told me how, as Archbishop of Kraków, the future Pope had ordered that a lecture on 'Orwell's *1984* and contemporary Poland', banned by the authorities, should be delivered in church. In Warsaw, the irrepressible Władysław Bartoszewski, who had survived both Auschwitz and Stalinist prisons, informed me at the top of his voice over lunch in a crowded restaurant: 'We count on the collapse of the Russian empire in the twenty-first century!' What a contrast to craven East Germany.

Returning to West Berlin, I found that James had decided to leave. He asked if I would like to take over the lease of his flat at Uhlandstrasse 127. Although the war had done for the outer façade, now just an ugly cement rendering with strange tear-drop gouges for decoration, this was a fine old place inside. You walked up another marble staircase, under Wilhelmine plaster busts and a flower-strewing cherub, to a grey-painted wooden door. It opened into a long corridor, wide enough to take a grand piano and perhaps fifteen feet high. There were two smaller rooms off to the left, then three beautiful, large, high-windowed rooms, each connected to the next by a handsomely carpentered, high double-door. The previous tenants had been political refugees from Iran. They had now gone back to their – as they thought – liberated homeland, but above the big double-bed there was still a lurid poster proclaiming 'Death to the Shah!'

How could I resist such a place? So I took it on, saying farewell to my little commune in the Traunsteinerstrasse. The diary records my last sighting of Bernd, setting off for a business trip to East Germany. Although theoretically convinced that the German Democratic Republic was the better Germany, Bernd did not much like going there. On this occasion, his car was loaded with cans, jars, bottles, tubes and packets of Western provisions. 'You know the food over there is so bad,' he explained, 'and the *service* . . .' Goodbye, comrade.

The Uhlandstrasse flat was wildly expensive for a student. In fact, ever since I came to Berlin I had been enjoyably but rapidly spending a small inheritance left me by my paternal grandfather, a some-time President of the Institute of Chartered Accountants, whom I knew only from the stern black-and-white portrait photograph on the piano at my grandmother's house. I somehow don't think he would have approved of the fruits of his Victorian thrift being spent in Ax Bax, Romy Haags and Foofie's, let alone in Warsaw or Tirana.

The letters from my bank manager were now becoming a little stiff. To retrench a little, I started filling the flat with sub-tenants. First, in the two front rooms, came Isabella, the German girlfriend of my American flatmate from the Traunsteinerstrasse. Then came Daniel Johnson, palely handsome, Nietzsche in hand. He would burst through the double-doors of a morning, beaming, to tell me he had located another German pessimist. Finally, we took in Mel, a Polish sculptor, and his wife Dot. They had fled Poland, leaving everything behind, and sought political asylum in Germany. 'Poland good, Poland communist bad!' Dot explained in her pidgin German. I knew exactly what she meant. Drinking brandy for breakfast, and reading the bureaucratic German of the terms for a sculpture competition, Mel suddenly exclaimed '*Luftwaffe London!*' The sculpture he submitted for the competition showed a man and a woman clinging together, their backs turned against a frightening new world. Mel and Dot. Down the road, there were still the cafés and the pretty girls, whom Daniel would startle with remarks like: 'Have you noticed that Steiner uses the word "moment" in the Hegelian sense?'

At the end of 1979, I prepared to move from this cheerful tower of Babel to East Berlin, where I had been offered a place as a research student attached to the Humboldt University, under a new cultural agreement recently signed between Britain and East Germany.

BY THIS TIME, Oxford and London seemed very far away. Occasionally I would fly back to Britain for a few days, visit my parents, lunch at the *Spectator*, go to the theatre, have dinner with friends and struggle, as on so many subsequent returns, to answer the impossible, only half-interested question: 'What's it like . . . ?' I would take the train to Oxford, talk to my supervisor and buy some books at Blackwell's, then return to London to sit the Civil Service exams and, on a subsequent visit, to be interviewed for the Foreign Service.

Now 'Foreign Service' normally means diplomatic service. But in Britain it can also mean something slightly different: the secret service. Here's something I had not thought about for years until I set out to investigate the Stasi file. I have to dig deep into my memory, into my diaries, even into a dusty old suitcase stashed away under the eaves of our house, to recover the details and to reconstruct that distant me.

When I was nineteen or twenty years old and an undergraduate at Oxford, I was quite interested in the subject of spying. I was inspired by the true stories of daring exploits in the Second World War. Thirty years after the end of the war, the whole extraordinary history of British espionage at that time was at last being written, especially by some of the Oxford dons who had been involved in it. I had a growing sense that there was still a kind of war on, against Soviet communism rather than Nazi Germany. I was intrigued by the life-stories of the Englishmen who spied for the Soviet Union, Philby, Burgess, Maclean and the still unidentified 'fourth man'. I also loved the novels of Graham Greene – and spying was the main industry of Greeneland.

I used to talk about all this for hours with one particular undergraduate friend, over coffee in my rooms looking on to the Broad. His father, I later learned, worked for MI5. Not that this was an obsessive interest for me, as it clearly was for Graham Greene, but it was one among many, beside theatre, modern architecture, literature and politics.

Then I have a picture in my memory of the front quad of Exeter College on a beautiful sunlit morning. I am approached, somewhere on the Chapel side, by the Rector of the College, a large, genial, tweedy man. What exactly he said, in his confidential rumble, I cannot remember, but the gist of it must have been that he had heard that I might be interested in this sort of thing and should he perhaps have a word with someone in London?

Today, this seems to me more like the opening scene of a film than anything that actually happened in my own life. *'The sunlit quadrangle of an Oxford college, green turf, golden sandstone walls. A tweed-suited don walks round the quad. He stops a fresh-faced undergraduate beneath the Chapel. We hear their parting words,* "... a word with someone in London...", "Thank you Rector ..." *Cut to a bare office in London ...'*

In a folder buried in a suitcase under the eaves of our house, I discover a letter dated 8 June 1976. The letterhead gives the anonymous-sounding title of a section of the Foreign and Commonwealth Office not listed in any official publications, and an address in central London. 'I understand that you would be interested to learn about the possibilities of a career in Departments for which [the section] has a recruiting responsibility.' Encloses a form, suggests 'an exploratory talk'. 'Should you have to make a special journey to London I will of course refund your second class rail fare.' Signed with a name, a real name which I find again in the 1995 *Diplomatic Service List*.

Now I see a bare office, a faintly shabby, balding man, with a scar on his chin. Of the conversation I remember only that he made a great point of impressing upon me that a career in this service would bring no outward status or honours, no titles or gongs. At the time – aged twenty-one – I found this merely funny. I still find it funny, but I can now imagine slightly better what it might feel like to be a middle-aged member of that service, ostensibly a diplomat, watching your perhaps less able contemporaries, the proper diplomats, making their steady progress up the hierarchy – Counsellor, Minister, Ambassador – and up the Order of St Michael and St George: CMG, KCMG, GCMG, or, as the old joke has it, Call Me God, Kindly Call Me God, God Calls Me God. I look at my interviewer's own entry in the 1995 *List*, and find five successive postings as First Secretary. Nobody calls him God.

I was, anyway, too young for the service, and went back to studying History at Oxford. According to my dusty folder, I reapplied shortly before leaving for Berlin in the summer of 1978. I even have a photocopy of my application forms. Under 'Main interests (political and social activity, principal reading, arts, sciences)', I find: 'International affairs; the two Germanies; Eastern Europe . . . Principal reading: Current affairs & contemporary history; modern European literature; English literature and general criticism; press.' I also confess my membership of the Society for Anglo-Chinese Understanding, a mildly fellow-travelling organization which I had joined simply because I was interested in China. (My 'little red book' of quotations from Chairman Mao still sits on the shelf.) As character referees, I name the Rector, of course, then my great-uncle, Sir Hugh Linstead, a retired MP, and my godfather, a barrister, QC, and soon to be a High Court judge. Eminently respectable, respectably eminent.

When I sat the Civil Service examinations in autumn 1978 (' "Constructive Thinking" only accounts for 10 per cent of the marks', my diary notes), and then went for the so-called Civil Service Selection Board in early 1979, it was for both the diplomatic and the secret branches of the Foreign Service that I was applying. These were two of several options I was considering, as many recent graduates do, until life's die is cast. I then flew back from Berlin for one day, on 17 May 1979, to have an extended interview for the secret service. My diary notes only, '2½ hours. The Interview. A great game', and that I then returned, via an exhibition at the Royal Academy and a telephone call to Melvin Lasky (editor of *Encounter* and a veteran cold warrior), to Berlin, 'disturbed by the Interview'.

Thinking back, I see a room somewhere in Whitehall, deep carpet, red leather, dark wood, some men sitting behind a table. Among them I recognize a senior Oxford history don. All I recall of the actual interview is a passage where I was asked to pretend to be a British 'diplomat' meeting a possible contact in a restaurant or bar in Barcelona. The contact was played by one of the men behind the table, and the only thing I distinctly remember of this make-believe conversation is myself saying, at frequent intervals, 'Have another drink'. This seemed to please the board.

In my folder, however, I find a further scrawled note on this meeting. The note is partly illegible, but beside mention of 'the Barcelona spiel', I find something about Libya and 'views on Eurocommunism' and then the stark entry: 'Betraying a Friend'. Was I asked the old question about choosing between betraying a friend and betraying your country, or what?

From my diary, it seems that I flew back from Berlin on 11 June 1979 for a medical check and security examination in the headquarters of the Secret Intelligence Service (SIS, often known as MI6), then an anonymous office block just south of the River Thames, and for lunch at a restaurant called 'South of the River'. Of this visit I remember little except the reception area and offices that were remarkable because they were so unremarkable. Grey filing cabinets, crowded desks, nondescript men in suits: like the housing department of Wandsworth Borough Council.

This time, however, my diary has more. Back in the communal flat in the Traunsteinerstrasse, I wrote down some impressions of 'the office, the firm, the service . . . The jolly secretaries and messengers. The doctor, [looking] like Malcolm Muggeridge . . . counselling a member on his alcohol problem. Amateurishness. Calculated shabbiness.' 'Briefing,' I note, 'with the rather absurd – but no doubt sharp – "Betty".' It seems Betty, 'looking slightly *scatty*', asked about my parents and brother: 'Are they *conscious?*'

I register the attractions: 'the GG element (GG for Graham Greene) . . . the mysteries. The sense of belonging to an élite. The challenge of the game.' But I am also very uneasy. Noting the suave, civilized manner of the officer who gave me lunch, I comment 'perhaps this is the (certainly less extreme) *English* version of *Goethe Oak*.' And then, with reference to my proposed journey through the Soviet bloc, his 'sinister and alarming phrase (let fall over the excellent Game Pie) . . . "we would rather have you under our control"'. The entry concludes: 'Returning on the plane, reading Bonhoeffer, discovering – rediscovering – the intellectual appetite, I am almost decided in my own mind which way to jump.'

However, the last document in my folder is the copy of a letter, datelined Traunsteinerstrasse, 21 June 1979, in which I merely write that 'I should like to postpone joining the service until September 1980'. A cautious move, still keeping the options open. But then I set off to drive for two months through-out the Soviet bloc – under no-one's control. The last entry I can find on the subject in my diary is from November 1979, and reads: '"We want you under our control". So no.' I had, therefore, clearly decided against joining before I went to East Berlin.

In Britain, ties with the secret service have long had a slightly *risqué* glamour. Well-known writers, biographers and historians have had well-known past connections with the service, from Somerset Maugham to Alistair Horne and Hugh Trevor-Roper. That was part of the attraction to the undergraduate me. But coming to it now through the Stasi file, and after years of immersion in Central Europe, I am slightly less amused. Even though I never joined, I imagine trying to explain to a Czech or Polish friend, for whom 'secret service' immediately sounds like 'secret police', how I could even have contemplated it; the difficulty, the near-impossibility, of making them truly under-stand how it all looked then, to an Oxford undergraduate from the strange breeding-ground of an English public school. Just as they would find it difficult to explain some things to me, without travelling back far into the half-forgotten realms of childhood.

In the beginning . . . was it Kipling's *Kim*, read as a child? Perish the cliché, but it may be true. The romance of the 'great game' on the north-west frontier of India certainly seemed closer to me because my maternal grandfather had served the Empire in the Indian Civil Service. When I visited them, my grandparents would enchant me with their own tales from the Raj: the jungle rides on elephants, a tiger jumping over the lane as they walked to the Club.

Then, most certainly, there were my father's memories of war, his stories of landing with the first wave on the Normandy beaches in 1944, my mother taking me aside – aged, what? Six? Seven? – and showing me the citation for his Military Cross: '... in the bitter and continuous fighting in the Normandy bridgehead his coolness and disregard of danger were quickly apparent ... His conduct, bravery and devotion to duty throughout the whole campaign are worthy of the highest praise ...' For all their formulaic stiffness, the words still move me deeply.

There follows the 'character-building' experience of being sent away from home at the age of eight to traditional, boys-only English boarding schools. The remembrance day service at St Edmund's; the cold steps up to Chapel at Sherborne, with the names of the war dead chiselled into the walls; daily imbrication with the rhetoric of patriotism, service, sacrifice; real-life war heroes coming back for Commemoration. Add Kipling, again ('he travels fastest who travels alone'); ripping yarns by John Buchan; even, in a curious way, the adolescent Tolkien phase; and just a little, I suppose, of Ian Fleming's two-dimensional, cardboard Bond. Add, too, the everyday laws of survival in boarding-school life, which required you to learn, very young, both self-reliance and the habits of secrecy, like Kim.

How to explain any of this to someone who never experienced it?

I can well understand how people came to join. Given the nature of the secret world, only they can say what it was really like in there – and they are not allowed to. Still, even without knowing exactly what I missed, or avoided, I am very relieved that I did not. I would fight against communism, but in my own way, as a writer.

I then had no further contact at all with MI6; or at least, I should more cautiously say, no conscious contact. From time to time, as I travelled around different countries, I casually reflected that the Nigel or Dick or Catherine from the British Embassy, who had just so genially offered me lunch or a drink, was perhaps a spy. Doubtless one or two of them were, but they were certainly not telling me – and anyway, I found it much more interesting to talk to the locals.

Yet such is the myth that surrounds the British secret service that British journalists, writers and scholars working abroad are very often thought to be spies. Those German journalists in West Berlin suspected that James Fenton, of all people, might be a spy, and it was not just the Stasi who suspected me. So, for example, did Polish friends I made in Berlin. Meanwhile, James and I sat in a bar idly wondering whether Stephen X. or Kevin Y. did not, perhaps, do a little work on the side for MI6. In many cases, this was probably idle gossip, put about by some hostile agency or malicious rival, or just the product of imaginations stirred by the myth. But in some cases it must have been true. Some 'journalists' and 'students' were more than they seemed.

So I am not surprised or outraged that the Stasi decided to take a closer look at me. What is shocking is the way they were spying on their own people and getting them to spy on each other: that vast army of surveillance, intimidation and repression, in which 'Schuldt', 'Smith', 'Michaela' and the rest were just a few foot soldiers. But the mere fact of this investigation of me is, in itself, still just about within the range of a 'normal' security service's work. In a lecture delivered in 1994, shortly after I started work on this book, the then head of Britain's Security Service (MI5), Mrs Stella Rimington, observed: 'Some governments will try every means – including enrolling their students at British universities – to bypass international agreements to obtain what they want. We are now working closely with others to identify and prevent their efforts.'

Moreover, while I had no secret agenda for the British government, I did have a secret agenda of my own. Using a pseudonym in the *Spectator*, and obviously not telling the East German authorities what I was up to, I was collecting material about the East German dictatorship. And the more I learned, the more I disliked it. Was I making secret preparations for attempted literary subversion? I certainly was.

To a communist state like East Germany, built on total control of the media, censorship and organized lying, any probing research or critical journalism was subversive. Western journalists were routinely covered by Stasi counter-intelligence department II/13. Partly this was because they were looking for spies under journalistic cover, but it was also because, for the Stasi, the distinction between journalist and spy was not clear-cut. For them, a Western journalist and a Western spy were both agents of Western intelligence-gathering and both alike threats to the security of the communist system.

Of course, all governments are always tempted to stifle awkward inquiry and to demonize critics as 'subversive'. Western governments often erred in this direction during the Cold War. Still, what I was doing in East Germany would never have been considered 'subversion' in West Germany, Britain or America. The difference was not, to be sure, between the pure white of a completely free press and the solid black of a wholly unfree one, but between the light grey of the largely free and the dark grey of the largely unfree. In East Germany, that grey was pretty dark.

For me, unlike for the Stasi, there is a very sharp line between working secretly as a spy for a government and working (sometimes secretively) as a writer. Yet there are still disconcerting affinities between the two pursuits. The proximity is even indicated in the language. The title of the West German secret service, the *Bundesnachrichtendienst*, translates literally as 'federal news service'. Conversely, some of the earliest German news-papers were called *Intelligenzblätter*, 'intelligence sheets', and the first issue of the nineteenth-century *Spectator* proclaimed that 'the principal object of a newspaper is to convey intelligence'. As the man from *Spekta*, I was a spy for 'intelligence' in that older sense. A spy for the reader.

I was far from alone in this. Many journalists writing about dictatorships do similar things and most journalists do some of them. And not just journalists. Writers of other kinds also find themselves in this territory. In his autobiography, Graham Greene reflects that 'every novelist has something in common with a spy: he watches, he overhears, he seeks motives and analyses character, and in his attempt to serve literature he is unscrupulous'. But how unscrupulous may he be? What means are justified to serve the end of 'literature'?

III

THE EVENING BEFORE I finally passed through the Wall I
threw a party for the friends and acquaintances I had made in
West Berlin, opening the high double-doors which linked the
rooms of the flat at Uhlandstrasse 127. According to my diary,
I finally went to bed at quarter to five in the morning on Monday
7 January 1980, got up again at a quarter past six, finished
packing, wrote a few last letters and then drove through Checkpoint Charlie and the East German frontier post ('all smiles'),
along a snowbound Unter den Linden, past the Alexanderplatz
and up the Schönhauser Allee to my new home in the working-
class borough of Prenzlauer Berg, Erich-Weinert-Strasse 24.

On the file, IM 'Schuldt' reminds me how it looked. Typing
neatly, single-space, he records: 'It is a relatively small room
(for an older building) with a window giving on to the street.
The door to the room is closed from inside with a security lock
which appears to have been fitted only recently. Apart from a
bed, a table and a pair of chairs, one notices above all a large
sideboard on which the tenant has – as I discovered – mainly
put books. Newspapers were laid out on the table (I noticed
above all several copies of "Sonntag") on which marginalia bore
witness to intensive reading. Beside them were several diction-
aries.' What he didn't remark upon, perhaps because he was
so used to it, was the general dinginess, the ochre walls, the
brown linoleum on the floor, the cheap plastic lampshade and
the freezing winter cold.

In this room, with the dark bulbous sideboard, I lived for

nine months, leaving East Berlin on 7 October 1980, the 31st anniversary of the foundation of the German Democratic Republic. The anniversary was as usual marked by a military parade, which – as usual – the Western allies vainly protested was in violation of the four-power status of Berlin, agreed with the Russians in 1945 and still theoretically in force. On my way to watch the parade, I met a cheerful black American GI wandering across the Alexanderplatz with a huge teddy bear, a souvenir of the Moscow Olympics. While giggling Young Pioneers, the communist girl guides and boy scouts, handed chocolates and flowers to the soldiers of the 'Friedrich Engels' Guards Regiment, I saw a British officer in khaki uniform and green beret leaping around with a portable step-ladder, filming the whole affair. Later, the Engels Guards marched off with carnations stuck in their rifle barrels.

The history books record that the period from January to October 1980 saw a further intensification of the East-West conflict. In May, West Germany reluctantly joined the American-led boycott of the Moscow Olympics in protest against the Soviet occupation of Afghanistan – although the American message had apparently not got through to that GI on the Alexanderplatz. At the end of August, a wave of strikes in Poland culminated in the deputy prime minister signing an agreement with the strikers at the Lenin Shipyard in Gdańsk. This agreement accepted the workers' right to form independent trades unions, a concession unprecedented in the history of communism. The new union would be called Solidarity. Some writers have referred to 'the making of the Second Cold War' – a striking phrase which, however, overlooks the fact that the Cold War had never really ceased.

My own life now began to engage directly with this outward history. First in East Germany, then in Poland during the Solidarity revolution, public and private intertwined. The physical distance from my large flat in the West to my small room in the East was less than ten miles; the psychological distance was several thousand. I popped over to the West quite often: my file records the precise date and time of every single border-crossing. West Berlin friends telephoned or came to see me in my dingy quarters.

Yet I find myself earnestly noting, just ten days after going to live in the East: 'I have something more than an indifference to [word illegible] contacts with my West Berlin life . . . It is an *active aversion*. Why? Because most of their concerns are (relatively) not *important*. It is *important* that human beings are diminished and mangled in the name of Equality and Peace and Justice. It is *important* that someone is sent to prison for years simply for wanting to leave the state in which he happens to have been born. It is important what happens in Afghanistan.' And a month later, after a telephone call from Irene: 'Ach, *that* world, of telephone "relationships" and eternal "relationship" problems.'

In East Berlin, I was still meant to be working on my thesis about Berlin in the Third Reich. The file contains references written by my Oxford mentors, Tim Mason and Tony Nicholls, for the British Council, which had arranged my stay as the first visiting research student under the new cultural agreement. Tim Mason was an inspiring teacher and, most unusually among Oxford historians, a Marxist, though of a distinctly unconventional, English-empirical kind. Indeed, he plainly did not qualify as a Marxist in the Stasi's judgement, for he is assessed in my file as writing 'from a bourgeois democratic position'. On the wall of his room in St Peter's College hung a poster showing Marx and Engels declaring 'Everyone's talking about the weather – we don't!' This perfectly summed up Tim Mason's bottomless contempt for English middle-class triviality, his high seriousness and painfully acute puritan work ethic. Tragically, he would take his own life some years later.

I am touched – with a sense of obligation – to read Tim's warm letter of recommendation. I fear he and Tony Nicholls were subsequently disappointed that I did not complete my doctoral thesis on Berlin under Hitler, but I think they saw the point of what I did instead. At its best, the Oxford history school has been tolerant of variety, even of eccentricity. 'In History's house are many mansions', the then Professor of Modern History, Richard Cobb, himself a full-blooded explorer of the outermost frontiers of the discipline, used crypto-biblically to declare at one of his not always entirely sober, sparsely attended, yet, for me, utterly entrancing lectures, delivered in some inspissated corner of the Taylorian Institution on a dismal Friday afternoon.

In fact, I did continue to spend time in the archives, but the East German authorities gave me only very restricted access to the relevant files. The main reason was probably that a full reading of the Nazi records would have shown how relatively small, and perhaps also how penetrated by the Gestapo, had been the communist resistance to Nazism; whereas the East German state was built upon the myth of a large communist-led 'anti-fascist resistance'. I also worked at the old Prussian State Library on Unter den Linden, in the so-called Special Research Department, which contained all the books and journals that the state did not want its ordinary citizens to read. It was known colloquially as 'the poison cupboard'. While I read yellowed copies of the Nazi newspaper *Völkischer Beobachter*, a senior officer of the 'Felix Dzerzhinsky' Guards Regiment, the military arm of the Stasi, sat at the next table studying copies of a West German illustrated news magazine and a Western armaments journal.

As my glance strayed from the Nazi newspaper to the Stasi officer, so altogether my attention was shifting from Hitler's Germany to Honecker's. I now firmly planned to write a book about the current German dictatorship. Communist austerity brought a distinct simplification of everyday life: one small room instead of five large ones, one kind of heavy, black bread in the gloomy state-owned corner-store, rather than the twenty different kinds of bread, roll, croissant and pastry at the baker's near my flat on the Uhlandstrasse. Helped by this enforced simplicity, I became more single-minded and set out to gather all the information I could.

IM 'Schuldt' rightly observed that I studied the press closely. I watched television, listened to the radio, read the more adventurous current fiction, which was also a partial substitute for the lack of a free press, and went often to the theatre. The Berliner Ensemble had now become little more than a Brecht mausoleum, but at the Deutsches Theater or the Volksbühne I found the kind of sly cultural resistance so familiar from my studies of Berlin in the 1930s. Sometimes it was the very same theatres, and even the same texts. I remember, for example, an electrifying reading of extracts from Heine's *Germany: A Winter's Tale* at the Deutsches Theater:

> I saw the Prussian soldiers again.
> They're still the same as ever.

Loud laughter.

> And still they strut about as stiff,
> As straight and thin as a candle,
> As if they'd swallowed the corporal's stick
> Old Fritz knew how to handle.

> The stick has never quite been lost,
> Although its use has been banned.
> Inside the glove of newer ways
> There's still the old iron hand.

I made full use of my unusual freedom of movement, as a research student with a visa for the whole country, by contrast with the accredited correspondents for Western newspapers, who had to ask permission to travel outside the city limits of Berlin and were presumably followed more intensively than I was. My diary laments horrendous repair bills for the car as I drove throughout the country on pot-holed roads. To Leipzig for the trade fair, where I first saw at close quarters the Party leader, Erich Honecker, and was astonished by how small he was. To Dresden on the anniversary of the February 1945 Anglo-American bombing of the city: '*Ach*, why did you do it?' asked one middle-aged woman in a café. To Greifswald, to visit my friend Rolf-Achim Krüger, now studying medicine there; to the Baltic island of Ruegen; to Schwerin, with Andrea and her ex-husband, for a very bad performance of Goethe's *Faust*. Then as often as possible to the wooded hills of Thuringia, my favourite of all the German lands, and of course to Weimar, that best and worst place in German history. Back in the capital, I went with a Polish friend to the Ballhaus Berlin, a dance-hall that still had numbered table-telephones. Spotting some pretty women, we dialled their number. But this was East Berlin, so the telephone didn't work.

Usually, though, I managed to talk to people wherever I went, and afterwards wrote down what they had told me. There were initial barriers of suspicion, heightened by fear of the Stasi. I have not projected this fear backwards on to the experience; this was something friends kept warning me about at the time. In Schwerin we were told: 'Watch out! The actor playing Faust works for the Stasi.' The narks swarmed like bluebottle flies at the trade fair in Leipzig. Rolf-Achim even wondered whether my car was bugged, as we drove down the autobahn singing the Wolf Biermann protest songs he had taught me. 'The green bursts from the branches,' we sang, as we sped through the night, 'then they'll know the score!'

I ate often at my local corner pub in Prenzlauer Berg, a

place of varnished wood and decrepit waitresses. Since seats in restaurants and pubs were invariably scarce, I usually had to share a table. Once, while I drank my beer and waited for a greasy Wiener Schnitzel, three young workers at my table were complaining loudly about their military service. Suddenly they stopped talking and looked suspiciously at this silent but keenly listening tablemate. An informal interrogation began, led by a thickset, muscular man with one finger missing on his right hand and wearing a University of California T-shirt. 'All right, so you say you're a historian,' he barked. 'Tell me, where was Karl Marx born?' Fortunately I knew the right answer. 'OK, who was leader of the KPD [the German communist party] in 1930?' Right again. 'Ummm, who brought Hitler to power? And' – he could no longer restrain himself – 'don't say the fucking monopoly capitalists.'

My English cheque card finally disarmed their suspicion. Then California apologized, and told his story. He was now twenty-two. His parents lived in West Berlin. On the night the Wall went up, the three-year old boy happened to be staying with his grandparents in the East. The East German authorities did not let him out again. He had subsequently been placed with foster parents, lost his finger during military service and now worked as a lorry driver. Sometimes his father would come over from West Berlin to visit, bringing a small present in his latest gleaming Mercedes. Hence the University of California T-shirt.

That was his story. You may find it incredible, and no doubt there were important details – perhaps a complicated family situation – which he did not tell me. Yet a lawyer involved in these cases has estimated that when the Wall went up in August 1961 there were as many as 4,000 children separated from their parents. A confidential report which I recently found among the papers of Chancellor Willy Brandt suggested that in August

1972 the GDR was still holding more than a thousand such children. So California's story may well have been true: he was one who didn't get away.

In any case, his hatred of the system was profound. 'Afghanistan?' he said. 'The Americans should march in from Pakistan and drive out the Russians.' They would need an invitation, of course, but the Russians had shown how that could be arranged. Look at the Czechoslovak communists' invitation to the Soviet Union to 'save' Czechoslovakia in 1968, or Babrak Karmal's recent invitation to do the same for Afghanistan.

Down the Erich-Weinert-Strasse, in a back courtyard garret, lived an acquaintance from the mildly dissident artistic scene of Prenzlauer Berg. He wore a permanent two-day stubble, and wrote poems and music. I christened him 'the young Brecht'. As a schoolboy in 1968, he and some friends had organized, in protest against the Soviet invasion of Czechoslovakia, a reading of Brecht's wonderful anti-Nazi resistance song from *Schweyk in the Second World War*:

> But time can't be halted. The boundless ambition
> Of those now in power is running its course.
> Like bloodspattered cocks they will fight for position
> But time can't be halted. Not even by force.

In an excited letter to a friend he then wrote: 'we are forming a resistance group.' For this, he was condemned to two-and-a-half years in prison, of which he actually served fifteen months. By the time he was released, his mother had emigrated to the West. She was not allowed back to visit him; he was not allowed out to see her.

He won a place to study at the Humboldt University, but as an ex-prisoner was disqualified from taking it. Then he himself applied to emigrate. He was refused. His wife left him. Now he worked three days a week in a cemetery, and spent the rest of his time in the bohemian milieu of Prenzlauer Berg. I remember the correspondent of a leading liberal West German paper, who also knew Young Brecht, telling me she thought he had made a rather happy little life for himself behind the Wall.

California and Young Brecht were extreme cases. More typical were the nice couple from whom the University had rented my room. Intelligent, well-educated, well-informed through watching Western television, they nonetheless devoted virtually all their energies to their private lives, and particularly to extending, decorating and maintaining their cottage on a small lake some half-an-hour's drive from Berlin. They had rebuilt the place with their own hands, including, as they proudly showed me, an electric water-pump, a roofed veranda, spotlights for evening table-tennis, a small private pier and a motorized rubber-dinghy.

My friend Andrea, too, concentrated on private life, bringing up her small children in the charmed atmosphere of a run-down old villa on the very outskirts of Berlin. There were lazy afternoons in the garden, bicycle-rides, sailing and swimming in the lakes. Modest idylls, especially for children. 'Inner emigration' and 'the unpolitical German' are the large phrases behind which such lives disappear.

I deliberately did not seek the company of Western correspondents, partly because I wanted to find out for myself and partly because I thought this might arouse the authorities' suspicions. However I did, perhaps incautiously, see quite a lot of Mark Wood, the Reuters correspondent. A loop of old-fashioned yellowing telex tape hung from a nail on the wall of the gloomy Reuters office on the Schönhauser Allee. It was an obituary of Hitler's deputy, Rudolf Hess, then the only Nazi prisoner of the wartime allies remaining in the Spandau fortress. Mark's predecessors in this office had included the thriller writer Frederick Forsyth, who had written a famous Reuters news story. On his way back to the office late one night in April 1964, he had seen Russian tanks rolling into the city centre. He telexed to London a dramatic, urgent story – an 'eight bells snap', which, on those old-fashioned telex machines, meant that a bell actually did ring eight times at the other end – and then went out to investigate. Only when news of the impending Third World War had been flashed around the world did he realize that these were just preparations for the regular 1 May parade. He was soon withdrawn from the Berlin office.

One snowy day in January, Mark and I drove out to look at the walled and closely guarded settlement at Wandlitz, where the top Party leadership lived in villas set among special shops and extensive gardens. The young guard at the gate noted down our passport details. When, feigning innocence, we asked him what this compound was, he nervously replied 'it's nothing'. The senior officer then informed us that it was 'a military object'.

On the file, I find a report from the head of Main Department PS (Personal Security, responsible for the security of the leadership) to the head of department XX/4. Describing the Party leaders' self-made ghetto as 'the residential object of the leading representatives', it records that we appeared at 17.55 hours in a dark green Alfasud (dark blue, actually), asked the way to a restaurant in Wandlitz and at 18.15 hours were 'banished from the object'. It also notes, unsurprisingly, that Mark was being covered by II/13 (journalists), while I was still with XX/4 (churches), in connection with the Reverend Beech-tree.

As we sat up at 1 a.m., drinking in the flat next to Mark's office, the telephone rang. Heavy breathing, then the line went dead. Half-an-hour later, the phone rang again and a voice said: 'I see you have a guest.' We guessed they were bored, or simply wanted us to go to bed. Knowing the place to be bugged, we took pleasure in loudly deploring the latest article by 'Edward Marston', my pseudonym in the *Spectator*. 'Did you see Eddie

Marston's latest piece, Tim?' 'Yes, terrible wasn't it? He must have been drunk again.' I ask Frau Schulz to enquire if there is a file on this enemy of the people but, alas, the central card index has no entry under Marston, Edward.

Mark, who today is Editor-in-Chief of Reuters, was told after unification that the next-door flat had been a Stasi surveillance centre, with wires from a control panel leading to a number of bugs planted in the wall of the Reuters flat, including several in the bedroom. They also had a visual observation post across the street. In technical coverage, the Stasi consistently outdid all but the wildest Western fantasies.

My favourite place of all, and a refuge from the general grey-ness and conformity, was Werner Krätschell's vicarage. A large man with a broad, strong-boned, truly Lutheran face and a deep, musical voice, Werner came from a long line of Prussian soldiers and priests. When the Wall went up, in August 1961, he was a twenty-one-year-old theology student and, illegally, on holiday in Sweden. After long discussions with his brother, he finally decided to return to the East. A group of West Berlin students, who were frantically forging identity papers for people to get out of East Germany, now rather bemusedly helped Werner to forge papers so he could get back in without being detected, since officially he was still there. Today, he says that he can only half disentangle the real mixture of motives for his extraordinary decision to go back, but one motive was a sense that 'he would be needed there' more than in the West.

He was certainly needed there. As a parish priest he offered pastoral care in a society which needed it at least as much as any other, despite the state's ideological claim to provide total welfare from cradle to grave. Later, as Dean of Pankow, he was increasingly called on to look after those who sought out the church as a space of freedom where you could speak a few truths, rather than as a place of Faith in revealed Truth.

Over coffee or a glass of wine, Werner would tell me, in his rich, slightly old-fashioned German, about his efforts to negotiate with officials of the party-state. Steeped in the tradition of Dietrich Bonhoeffer and the anti-Nazi Confessing Church during the Third Reich, he still believed that a dialogue with the communists could bear fruit. Yet he also told me about the repression and the costs that his own family bore. Like many clergymen's children, his eldest son, Joachim, was not even allowed a normal secondary education.

I treasured these conversations and the warm, tranquil atmosphere of the old vicarage. Occasionally we would go out together for a meal or a lecture, or to drive through the Brandenburg countryside with Fontane's *Travels around the Mark Brandenburg* as our guidebook. So little had changed in a hundred years!

Several of my meetings with Werner are described in observation reports: some now in my file, some in his, some in both. The shortest of these is on 17 October 1979, when a nark picked me up at Friedrichstrasse at 18.35 but lost me by 18.45. According to my diary, I was off to a reading by the communist writer Stephan Hermlin.

For 27 February 1980 they record a visit paid by 'Romeo', 'Beech-tree' and his son to the City Library: '17.40 hours "Beech-tree" parked his Wartburg in front of the building. The three persons then entered the City Library. They checked their coats into the cloakroom and proceeded to the lecture room on the second floor. Here they listened to a lecture on Prussian history and Prussiandom.' Some might say that this nark's report was itself another small page in the history of Prussiandom, although Werner, with his romantic attachment to the Prussian heritage, is still reluctant to accept this.

In Werner's own file I find the same report but also, carefully preserved in a buff envelope, some black and white photographs of us entering the City Library – presumably taken with a concealed camera. There is Werner, with his large frame and broad, strong features. He was forty then, the age I am now. There is young Joachim, a little figure with curly side-locks, looking uncannily like one of the small Jewish boys in Roman Vishniac's haunting photographs of the vanished world of East European Jewry before 1939. Joachim was twelve years old then, the age my eldest son is now. And there am I, aged twenty-four, fresh-faced, still clean-shaven, hair short and parted almost in the centre, tweed jacket, with a silk handkerchief in the top pocket, cord trousers and doubtless those Oxford shoes.

My diary records the previous thirty-six hours in the life of this earlier self, this me/not me. A Polish lesson in the morning. Then a call at the Albanian Embassy: 'Albanian raki and conversation', the diary says, cryptically. Drop in to the British Embassy to collect my post, which was delivered there for me, as for several British people living in East Germany, because it seemed likely to be quicker and safer. A few hours' reading. Dinner at Stockinger, a restaurant on the Schönhauser Allee, with Ursula von Kardorff, a hugely spirited survivor of wartime Berlin who was working on a new guidebook to the city. Turning aside from the diary, I take the Kardorff guidebook down from my bookshelf and read '*Stockinger* . . . typical GDR-style rusticity with pretentious cuisine'.

Later in the evening, across to West Berlin, 'over Charlie'. First to the Paris Bar, then off to the Kurfürstendamm flat of a lady called Ingrid Schick and 'red wine and rowdy argument from about 10 p.m. to 5.15 a.m.' From there, straight to an early breakfast at 'Mau Mau', an all-night café. Back across the frontier to East Berlin, getting home shortly before 7 a.m., 'meeting on the stairs a frontier guard, just off to do his day's work'. Two hours' sleep. Some work in the library. A meeting with Dr Demps, the 'adviser' assigned me by the university.

Then off with Werner and Joachim to that lecture on Prussia and Prussiandom. Afterwards we had dinner at Stockinger again. And so to bed.

Werner would became a dear friend. When my first child was born some years later, Werner became his godfather: Uncle Werner, behind the Wall. We have worked together on the research for this book. Shortly after unification, he met Colonel Wiegand, the senior Stasi officer responsible for the churches. Wiegand began the conversation by telling him that they had been especially interested to listen to a telephone call which Werner had made to me in Oxford from a friend's flat in West Berlin, on one of the rare occasions when he had been allowed out. Werner had assumed that it was safe to telephone from the West, but apparently they could get a fix on any number in West Berlin. For calls between West Berlin and West Germany they had a sophisticated listening station located, suitably enough, on the Brocken mountain, scene of the fabled witches' sabbath or Walpurgis Night. Their equipment could be programmed to record any conversation in which a particular word or name was mentioned.

By August 1980, I had collected enough material to start writing. After saying farewell to Andrea, I took the train to Italy, where I began work on the book while staying with my friends Sally and Graham Greene. I was deeply frustrated by the Western accounts of East Germany that appeared at this time, often produced by '68ers revolting against what they saw as the crude anti-communism of the older generation. The word 'Stasi' – or 'State Security Service' or 'secret police' – did not appear at all in the twenty-page index to the best general book about East Germany then published in Britain. Instead, Jonathan Steele's *Socialism with a German Face: The state that came in from the cold* concluded that East Germany's 'overall social and economic

system is a presentable model of the kind of authoritarian welfare states which Eastern European nations have now become'.
But presentable to whom? Not, I found, to most of the East
Germans I met. I had no partisan agenda of Right against Left.
My objection to these descriptions was not that they were Left
but that they were wrong – inaccurate, partial, patronising, deaf
to the plain truths that the people who actually lived there could
tell you. I wanted to describe it as it really was.

This description included the Stasi. 'Suspicion is everywhere,'
I wrote. 'It strikes in the bar, it lurks in the telephone, it travels
with you in the train. Wherever two or three are gathered
together, there suspicion will be.' I quoted Western estimates
that there were at least 100,000 informers working for the secret
police. I was particularly interested in the way the communist
regime drew upon older German traditions and habits of
obedience.

After I had been writing for just a few days, the BBC World
Service reported that an occupation strike had begun at the
Lenin Shipyard in Gdańsk. Italian newspapers printed grainy
photographs of a moustachioed worker called Lech Wałęsa. I
knew at once that I simply had to be there. I cut short my
holiday and took the train back to Berlin. Sitting in the station
buffet at Munich, I read a report in *Le Monde* of how the strikers
had refused the government's offer of a special supermarket
instead of the monument they demanded to commemorate the
workers killed in the previous round of protest on the Baltic
coast. They preferred the symbol to the food. Early on the
Monday morning, I went to the Polish embassy in East Berlin
to get a visa, and soon I was inside the Lenin Shipyard.

I sat with the unshaven, exhausted strikers watching the end
of a communist party Central Committee meeting on television,
and when the Party leaders were seen standing up to intone the
Internationale, the people around me spontaneously rose to

their feet and began singing the Polish national anthem. 'Arise, ye prisoners of want,' piped the television. 'Poland is not yet lost,' thundered the strikers, 'so long as we live!' Their hands shot up, all making the 'V for Victory' sign. Yet in all our minds was the thought that Soviet tanks might again roll, as they had to crush the Prague Spring just twelve years before.

IV

THE SOURCES the Stasi themselves considered most important were the 'unofficial collaborators', the IMs. The numbers are extraordinary. According to internal records, in 1988 – the last 'normal' year of the GDR – the Ministry for State Security had more than 170,000 'unofficial collaborators'. Of these, some 110,000 were regular informers, while the others were involved in 'conspiratorial' services, such as lending their flats for secret meetings, or were simply listed as reliable contacts. The Ministry itself had over 90,000 full-time employees, of whom less than 5,000 were in the HVA foreign intelligence wing. Setting the total figure against the adult population in the same year, this means that about one out of every fifty adult East Germans had a direct connection with the secret police. Allow just one dependant per person, and you're up to one in twenty-five.

The Nazis had nothing like as many. In 1941, the full-time staff of the Gestapo, the Nazis's Secret State Police, for the vastly larger territory of Greater Germany, including Austria and what is today the Czech Republic, was less than 15,000. Even adding the Reich Security Service and other possibly comparable units, one still cannot reach anything like the Stasi proportions. We have no national statistics for the number of regular informers, but it seems clear that this was also very much smaller. Over its relatively short life, starting with real popular enthusiasm and ending with five-and-a-half years of war, the Third Reich could rely much more on voluntary denunciations – as I found in those dusty People's Court files.

In East Germany, the regime was never popular to start with, and the longer it went on the more it came to rely on this huge network of informers.

I appear to have had the attentions of five. Their evidence and operational potential are carefully weighed by Lieutenant Wendt. As I study their reports on me, set out to identify, find and talk to them in person, I am drawn back not just into my own past life but into these other lives that briefly crossed with mine.

I was not a victim of these informers, as many East Germans really were of theirs. They did me no serious damage. Yet, knowing how the system worked, it is a fair guess that they did harm others. I cannot say how typical they are of Stasi informers in general, although I know enough of other cases to say that some elements are common. However, the fact that they happen to have informed on me gives me a special chance to test the accuracy of the files – and to enter into their own experience. Why did they do it? What it was like for them? How do they see it now?

I start with that 'IM of the HVA I – adviser of the G. at the H[umboldt] U[niversity] B[erlin]', who, according to the opening plan of action, is to be brought in to the 'operational treatment'. My adviser, Laurenz Demps, was someone I knew more than casually. He was a large, hearty Berliner, with an extraordinary knowledge of the city's history and a sharp side-line in black humour. I still have the handsome volume of Heinrich Zille drawings which he gave me as a leaving present. He was also a staunch Party member with a romantic nostalgia for the street-fighting days of the communists in Weimar Berlin.

The case interests me particularly because he is one of relatively few East German historians to have retained his position after the country was united with the West. In fact, he has been made a full Professor at the Institute of History in the Humboldt University, despite a rigorous purge of former staff by the new Western management. Before calling Laurenz Demps himself, I discuss the case with the Director of the Institute, Heinrich August Winkler, a distinguished West German historian, and with Stefan Wolle, an East German who refused to make the political compromises necessary to climb the academic career ladder under communism and now has to start again from a relatively humble position. They both point out that, unlike many of his colleagues, Demps has come unscathed through the university's extensive vetting procedures. These include, crucially, the prescribed enquiry to the Gauck Authority, known colloquially as 'being gaucked'.

Yet there would be an explanation for Laurenz Demps getting a clean bill of health from the Gauck Authority if he was an informer for Markus Wolf's foreign intelligence service, the HVA. For most of the records of that service have been destroyed – or in part, it is sometimes said, transported to Moscow. Klaus Eichner, a ruddy-faced former Colonel of the HVA, describes to me how already in the late autumn of 1989 they were busy shredding and burning the most sensitive files, and removing their agents' cards from the Ministry's central records. This temporarily stopped when the Stasi headquarters were occupied in mid-January 1990. But then, in an extraordinary decision of the Round Table negotiating the transition from communist rule, the foreign intelligence service, alone among all the departments of the Stasi, was formally empowered to continue its own 'self-dissolution'. So throughout the spring and early summer they went on destroying any files that would identify individual agents and informers. 'I was destroying my life's work with my own hands', says Colonel Eichner.

Names from two back-up copies of card indexes have since reached the West German authorities, and some of Wolf's senior officers have talked, thus producing evidence for a number of trials. But these sources mainly concern agents working in the West. That being so, an informer of the foreign intelligence wing will usually be exposed only if there happens to be a cross-reference in the files of other departments. Otherwise he or she will come through not as the life-threatening 'gauck-positive' but, like Laurenz Demps, as 'gauck-negative'. Another revealing colloquialism: having a Stasi past is like having Aids.

'For what it's worth,' says Stefan Wolle, who himself studied at the Humboldt in the 1970s, 'people used to say that Demps had something to do with the Stasi.' And then: 'Well now, if you want to hang him . . .' But he says it with a kind of wry weariness, and I hear behind his words: 'well, if you really must . . .' This from Stefan, who ever since the fall of communism has argued vigorously for a radical purge of former Stasi collaborators.

'Well now, if you want to hang him . . .' What a responsibility! With just eleven words in a file – 'an IM of the HVA I – adviser of G. at the HUB' – I can, if I choose, ruin a man's career, perhaps even his life. For IM is the kiss of death. What earthly right have I to play judge and hangman? And for what? The actual content of the two-page document headed 'copy of an IM report', passed to department II/9 by the HVA in July 1980, is wholly inoffensive. It ascribes to Dr Demps the view that I work purposefully and thoroughly, with a bourgeois-liberal attitude – although 'no commitment to the working class' – and concludes with the suggestion (wishful thinking, but perhaps encouraged by me) that he might come to Oxford as examiner of my thesis. It has done me no harm.

Only the clear identification of Demps as an informer makes the thing serious. If this is true, there is an argument of historical justice for at least reporting it to the university, from which other scholars have been purged for being informers. When I say 'purged' I should be more exact. They have not been banned from working altogether, just dismissed from this particularly sensitive position as university teachers; and by no means all those identified as informers have been sacked. According to the university's first West German rector, one in every six professors and one in ten university employees had worked for or in some way cooperated with the secret police under the old regime. Of these, many have left voluntarily and some seventy have been dismissed. But the university 'commission of honour' has also found in many other cases that the offence was not serious enough to merit dismissal. Clearly someone should not, in fairness, escape this rigorous but discriminating judgement just because of the historical accident that a particular set of files has disappeared.

None of which makes me any happier as I telephone Professor Demps, one day in June 1995, to arrange my appointment. I have had no contact with him since 1981. He is clearly surprised by my call and the news that I have 'something I want to discuss' with him, but agrees to meet. We fix a rendezvous in a café on the Wilhelmstrasse, about which he has just published a rather well-received book. His exceptional knowledge of Berlin's local history has also earned him a place on a prestigious commission to propose changes to East Berlin street names: Marx-Engels-Platz to be Schlossplatz, part of Karl-Liebknecht-Strasse to be Schinkelallee, part of Karl-Marx-Allee to be Hegelallee, and so on.

Eleven sharp, and there he sits outside the café, a large man with a pasty complexion and rheumy eyes, wearing grey trousers and a red pullover with epaulettes. A slightly tense greeting. Tea and coffee ordered. Then I come to the point. I have read my Stasi file and it would appear that they had him down as an informer of the HVA.

'*Au weia!*' says Laurenz Demps.

I explain what the file says and show him copies of the relevant pages. His hand shakes slightly as he takes the copies. When he lights a cigarette he spills the ash down the front of his sweater: 'You see how agitated I am.'

But no, he says, he was not an informer, he had nothing to do with the Stasi. 'Oddly enough, they never approached me.' However, he does remember talking about me to the head of the university's International Department. 'What was the man's name? You remember, we had lunch together once in the Operncafé?'

As soon as he says this, I see it all. I have been puzzled by the fact that the 'copy of an IM report' from the foreign intelligence service does not give the informer a code-name, but in mid-text identifies my adviser with his full-name: 'Com[rade]. Dr Laurenz [Name blacked out]' as it appears on this copy. However, I reasoned, if Lieutenant Wendt of Stasi counter-intelligence read this to mean that Demps was an informer for the foreign intelligence service, who am I to doubt it? Wendt must have known what he was doing. Perhaps foreign intelligence worked by slightly different rules from the rest of the ministry.

Now I see that it was that man from the university's International Department who was the informer – and someone in his position would obviously have had contacts of interest to Wolf's spies. What the foreign intelligence service has passed on is a copy of *his* report, hence the identification of Dr Demps by his real name. It is Lieutenant Wendt who has been sloppy in his work, eliding the informer and the informer's source.

As Demps pores over the report, he points out that, while much of the information obviously came from him, there are also things he did not know – such as my contact with Mr Wildash at the British Embassy. 'Look at this sentence', he says, and we both bend our heads over the document. Two historians discuss the interpretation of a primary source.

Now complete denial of the accusation is, I am told, the most usual first reaction of an IM. The denial sometimes continues long after the informer is confronted with incontrovertible evidence; denial, then, in a psychological as much as a criminological sense. But Laurenz Demps's reaction seems to me that of an innocent man and his explanation is immediately convincing. On my return to Oxford, I find that I still have my notes from that lunch in the Operncafé on (it appears) 27 March 1980. In these notes, I describe the head of the International Relations department as a 'Smart Alec/Flash Harry. Brown jacket. Loud tie. Sancho Panza mustache'. I note the somewhat forced mateyness of the two Party members, the demonstrative way they use the comradely *Du* to each other but the more formal *Sie* to me. Flash Harry had studied 'scientific communism' in Leipzig. 'You know there is a joke that does the rounds here,' he tells me confidentially, over another liqueur. 'We say "dictatorship of the proletariat". Now I can see the proletariat, but where is the dictatorship?' And so on. I'm glad to hear from Laurenz Demps that this nauseating man has long since left the University. I wonder what he's doing now?

But how did Demps himself see me at the time?

He points to the Stasi report: 'Much as it says here!' It was fairly interesting to have an English student, but, you know how it is, advising students always takes precious time away from your own research. And then he asks how I saw him.

As a convinced communist, I say, and as someone with an almost romantic view of the pre-war German Communist Party.

Yes, that's true, he replies, although adding that there were many things that one didn't say to a foreigner. According to my notes from 1980, what he did say to me at that lunch was: 'We don't expect you to join the Communist Party of Great Britain ... All we want is that you should take us seriously and tell people in the UK that we are serious people.' But then he added a personal aside: 'Will you spit on Churchill's grave for me?'

Probably it was little jokes like that which contributed to my lack of interest in looking up my old adviser after it again became possible for me to enter East Germany. But I have nothing but sympathy – and some admiration – for the way he copes with the shock I have just given him.

'I thought of all sorts of things when you telephoned,' he says, 'but never this.' In fact, he had recently been sent pages from a friend's file in which he himself appeared as a suspect, because he took a leading part in a private discussion group. Picking up my comment about romanticism, he muses 'yes, but romanticism can be dangerous'.

Then it's time for him to give some American students a guided tour of the Wilhelmstrasse. 'After this,' he says, 'I'm going to drink a large schnapps.' He is still visibly shaken, like a man who has stood for a moment under the gallows. Had he been a prominent public figure, and I an unscrupulous journalist, he could well have been 'hanged'. I can just see the report in *Der Spiegel* – how often in recent years have we read them – with the little inset black-and-white photograph of a page from the file, and the damning line circled in red: 'an IM of the HVA I – adviser of G. at the HUB.' Damning, but wrong.

For myself, I am just very, very relieved. I can hardly wait to get back to the hotel, to telephone Winkler and Wolle and explain the Stasi's mistake.

As I am finishing this book, Stefan Wolle faxes me a newspaper cutting about a newly founded Berlin-Brandenburg Prussian Association. Of the founding members, the report mentions only one name: 'Humboldt University historian Laurenz Demps.'

A telephone number is given, and when I ring up, the Prussian Association sends me an information pack. From this I learn that the Association is to cultivate the 'true values and virtues of Prussia' and to 'lay the foundation-stone for a spiritual renewal of our fatherland' since Germany threatens to degenerate into a 'multicultural assortment of intolerant individualists'. The Association's statute makes special mention of the 'philosophical writings of Frederick the Great'. Its keynote speaker commends the spirit of the King and his soldiers at the Battle of Leuthen in 1757. 'True Prussiandom', he says, is associated with patriotism, selflessness, tolerance, modesty, loyalty and a sense of duty, but also with 'secondary virtues such as punctuality, love of order and cleanliness'.

V

MY MOST ASSIDUOUS informer is 'Michaela', the lady in Weimar. On 9 February, the Erfurt office reports to counter-intelligence department II/13 (journalists) that I have again been in touch with their IMV 'Michaela'. Erfurt also encloses the transcript of a taped conversation with her husband, previously described as 'Georg' but now 'Michael'. In this transcript, Dr Georg recalls his experiences at Reuters in London, starting in 1943. As Joint Managing Editor of the European Desk, Dr Georg reports, he had great problems editing features written by such 'sworn Soviet-enemies' as 'Richard Löwenthal ... now professor of politics at the Free University in Berlin', Alfred Geiringer and the Swiss Jon Kimsche.

And so the Stasi file, this cardboard time-machine, transports me back not just fifteen but a full fifty years, to Britain at war. In fact, the three names he mentions could stand for those of many Central European exiles in London at that time: men and women who owed their freedom to Britain's solitary stand against Hitler and who subsequently gave much to Britain – and Europe – in return. Turn the page, and I might be reading about Arthur Koestler, or André Deutsch, or Sebastian Haffner, or George Mikes, or about another young Central European exile, then working as a news commentator on European affairs for the BBC's Empire and North American service, but now known to all the world as George, the Lord Weidenfeld, of Chelsea.

The communist Dr Georg had discussed his difficulties in

censoring the 'sworn Soviet-enemies' with Comrade Hans [name blacked out], who was in a similar position on *Time* magazine. His problem with editing those anti-Soviet commentaries, 'so that the most poisonous parts were removed', got worse towards the end of the war, he says, and he decided to contact the relevant section of the War Office in order to seek a position in post-war Germany. This he did 'with the agreement of our comrades – the leadership of the London group had in the meantime passed to Feliks Albin (Kurt Hager)'. (Kurt Hager would subsequently become one of the longest-serving members of the East German politburo and the Party's chief ideologist.) The War Office, in its wisdom, then entrusted this German communist with the job of building up 'the first [post-war Western] German news agency DENA in Hamburg'. The British officials' grasp of geography seems to have been as shaky as their political judgement, for Dr Georg also managed to persuade them that to go from London to Hamburg he needed to pass through Berlin.

So on 13 May 1946 he received his handwritten official permission to travel to Berlin. 'It had been agreed with the comrades in London that I should report to the C[entral] C[ommittee] ... The comrades on the spot should decide whether I should take up the Hamburg job or remain in Berlin.' After long discussions, they decided that he should stay in Berlin to build up the East Germany news agency, 'but then I ended up with the Soviet news agency in Weissensee'.

He wrote to the head of the embryonic Hamburg operation, explaining that he could not take up the job for political reasons, since he disagreed with British policy towards Germany. Dr Georg also recalls, with almost audible amusement, that as nothing had been heard from him for nearly two-and-half-weeks, British newspapers had run reports of his mysterious disappearance and speculated that he had been kidnapped by the Russians.

'Since my return to the then S[oviet] O[ccupation] Z[one],' the transcript concludes, 'I have had no close contact with any of the acquaintances connected with my London activities.'

Two touches must be added to this self-portrait of Dr Georg at war. The first concerns his then boss at Reuters, Christopher Chancellor. The transcript in my file records only that Dr Georg had learned that Chancellor was critical of his decision to leave Reuters, finding it 'arrogant'. While I was writing this book, I met Christopher Chancellor's son, Alexander Chancellor, my own former Editor at the *Spectator*, at a party given by the Editor of *The Times* for the Editor of the *New Yorker*. Amidst this clamour of Editors, I asked him if he had ever heard his father speak of one Georg [true name], and explained the circumstances. For a moment, the bitter taste of Central Europe's tortuous history intruded between sips of champagne on a beautiful summer's evening in a North London garden. Alexander punched the name into his computer notebook and said he would consult his elder brother. A couple of weeks later we met again and he told me the result of his enquiries. His brother did not know the particular name. However, he did remember that around that time their father had come home very worried and angry about revelations of Soviet spies at Reuters.

The other touch concerns Dr Georg's then girlfriend: Alice 'Litzi' Philby. Kim Philby had parted from the Jewish communist Litzi in 1936, at a time when he was posing as a sympathizer with fascism and supporting the Francoist side in the Spanish Civil War. Litzi, meanwhile, was living in Paris, and it seems that it was through her that Philby kept in touch with Soviet intelligence. In 1939, she moved to London and managed to bring her parents out of Vienna – just in time. In London, she got together with Dr Georg. Some mystery surrounds the circumstances in which she finally divorced Philby and left

England, but by 1947 she had joined Dr Georg in East Berlin and married him there, using her maiden name. Nine years later, they, in turn, were divorced. Dr Georg went on, after another marriage, to make his life with 'Michaela', and moved with her to Weimar. Litzi stayed in Berlin.

Early in my time in East Berlin I went to visit this woman whose life was a history of the twentieth century. We talked over afternoon tea and delicious Viennese macaroons in her small flat on the Karl-Marx-Allee. Her bookshelves contained Tennyson, Keats, the Oxford Book of English Verse and Ignazio Silone's *The School for Dictators*. My notes record a small, attractive, energetic woman with a Viennese accent and frizzy hair, 'very young for her age' – she was then seventy – and, as I rather oddly put it, 'inquisitive to a fault'. 'Soviet agent training?' I asked myself. 'Caution because of bad experience with foreigners posing as . . . ? Or simply, and in the end this is the hypothesis I prefer, Viennese bourgeois habit.' It was probably a mixture of all three. After her exciting youth, she had spent the last twenty years until her retirement dubbing foreign films for the state film distributor. She now enjoyed an excellent state pension as a 'fighter against fascism'.

She talked affectionately and admiringly about Kim. 'He was very brilliant', she said – the last two words spoken in English – and had a genius for languages. However he was, she added, 'somewhat reserved'. She was sure the Vienna workers' rising in 1934 and its brutal suppression had been a formative experience, turning him into a fully committed communist. In fact, she herself seems to have played a decisive role. It was through her that the young man from chilly old England was plunged into a new world of high political excitement, quick, warm friendships, seemingly uncomplicated solidarity and probably a fair dash of sexual liberation as well. It may also have been her who introduced him, in the midst of all this, to Soviet intelligence.

I felt I could hardly ask her about the sex. Instead, I asked her whether she and Philby would have chosen the path they did if they had known what was really happening in the Soviet Union in the 1930s. There was a long pause and then she said, very seriously, 'I really can't answer that. It must seem incredible to you that we didn't know about it all . . .'

What did she think of East Germany now?

'Well, let's say it is not what we hoped for or believed in.'

She criticized the general mistrust, the fearfulness and timidity of the leadership, the lack of freedom of expression and freedom of movement, and the privileges – even her own. However, she still believed in something she called socialism. 'What's the alternative? I see none.'

Back to the file. 'Michaela' reports that on 5 January 1980 she received from me a copy of an exhibition catalogue entitled *Between Resistance and Conformity: Art in Germany 1933–1945*. She confirms that the handwriting on the attached greetings card is the same as that on the piece of paper on which I had written down my name during my last visit. 'In order to implement further measures to strengthen the contact as well as *Blickfeldmassnahmen* [a special Stasi term meaning keeping someone in view] I will send a letter of thanks to the address given below:

Tim Gartow Ash

Kunstgalerie

Berlin-West.'

Underneath is typed 'Michaela'. The report is not signed by hand, but a note at the bottom seems to refer to an IM file.

Five months later a minute 'produced from verbal information given by IMV "Michaela"' reports that her husband had told her how, on the weekend of 26–27 April, I had tried to visit them again. Dr Georg had declined to see me, saying he was too ill. However, he had found out some details of my Weimar visit by asking the doctor who was looking after him at the time. The doctor happened to be married to Eberhard Haufe, 'a freelance scholar of German literature', and I had actually stayed with them.

I remember that weekend. These were the 'Shakespeare Days' in Weimar, and the main event was a lecture by George Steiner. It was a characteristic bravura performance, from Lear to *Twelfth Night* by way of Oedipus and *Don Giovanni*. Afterwards I had supper with the great man. I felt there was something particularly appropriate about talking to Steiner here in Weimar, in the shadow of Buchenwald – surely the quintessential example of that profoundly disturbing proximity of high culture and barbarism about which Steiner had written so eloquently. But my notes record little conversation on that subject: 'No, what he wanted to do was to *gossip* – and did so, relentlessly, unceasingly, *cascading* for over an hour over supper in the [Hotel] Elephant. Have you heard the latest about the Regius Professor? etc. "My, how you must miss it all!"' My notes express a disappointment which, today, I find just a little unfair; for after all, the sage had been talking very seriously about great matters all day.

Nonetheless, it was not Shakespeare and George Steiner but Goethe and Eberhard Haufe who made that weekend memorable.

> Wer den Dichter will verstehen
> Muss in Dichters Lande gehen.

To understand the poet you must visit his country, Goethe wrote, and no place in Europe is more eloquent of the writers who lived there than Weimar. First, his own house, with the wonderfully preserved library and his standing desk: Hebbel called it the only battlefield of which Germany could be proud.

Then Schloss Kochberg, where Goethe worshipped Charlotte von Stein, before bedding the more comfortable Christiane. On to Schiller's house, the tomb of the two poet-princes and the wonderful parks: On The Ilm and Tiefurt and that of Schloss Belvedere – the residence, two hundred years after the Duchess Anna-Amalia, of IM 'Michaela'.

The eloquence of the place was matched by the company of Eberhard Haufe and his family, with whom, as my diary records, I walked in the parks and visited Schloss Kochberg. Eberhard Haufe was a small, fragile man, with a precise and somewhat old-fashioned manner of speaking. Since his dismissal, for political reasons, from the University of Leipzig in the late 1950s, he had lived as a textual editor and critic, working on editions of the German classics and his special passion, Johannes Bobrowski, the poet of the European east.

As we walked, we had the kind of intense conversation about books, ideas and politics which I would often have with intellectuals and churchmen in Europe behind the iron curtain, but less often with their counterparts in the West. Here there was the added charm of being in Weimar with a scholar of the German classics and I felt, as we walked through the Tiefurt park, that the white-haired, delicate figure beside me was not just an expert on the intellectuals of classical Weimar; he was one of them. He stood in a continuum, and a conversation, which stretched back two centuries. A conversation which was and still is at heart about the true meaning of one central but elusive concept of German writers and thinkers from Herder to Thomas Mann: *Humanität*. (Literally 'humanity,' but with a very large 'H'.)

Unlike the East German guidebooks to Weimar, Dr Haufe had no illusion that *Humanität* was in any way embodied by the regime of the German Democratic Republic – though it put Goethe on its 20 Mark notes. This regime was, for him, the negation of *Humanität*. He told me about the Stasi opening letters and bugging telephone conversations, and about his own long struggles with the censors, who objected even to a book he had edited under the title *German Letters from Italy*. The GDR was endeavouring to implement Kurt Hager's ideological ruling that there was no longer a German nation, but rather a separate 'socialist nation' and 'capitalist nation' – hence the campaign to remove the adjective 'German' wherever possible, even from Dr Haufe's innocuous book title.

As a leaving present, he gave me a small volume he had edited. I have it before me as I write. Entitled *The Untimely Truth*, it contains aphorisms, short prose pieces and an essay 'on publicity' by a long-neglected early nineteenth-century German writer, Carl Gustav Jochmann. Coming from Riga, and inspired by his experience of living in England during the unsettled years 1812 to 1814, Jochmann makes a passionate case for the political importance of free speech. In an editorial postscript dated 1975, Haufe negotiates these subversive views past the East German censor with a fine double-edge: 'just because [Jochmann] spoke from the darkness of an underdeveloped, constricted bourgeois world, he spoke also and still with the innocent voice of intellectual integrity and yearning. Public opinion was not yet recognizable as "false consciousness", as a mask for the purely bourgeois class interest, as it was a half generation later for the young Marx.' His readers, with long experience of reading between the lines, got the message immediately, and the first edition sold out in no time.

On the flyleaf of my copy I find written in a tiny, neat hand: 'Where the truth must be fought, there it has already won, C. G. Jochmann. Believing in the truth of this and similar sentences, cordially dedicated to Timothy Garton Ash by Eberhard Haufe, Weimar, 27.IV.80.'

A delightful and rather moving visit then. But that is not how it appears in the Stasi report from' Michaela'. Here I appear as a rude and unwelcome guest: 'In the evening G. ignored discreet indications that the family H. regarded the conversation as concluded and he managed to ensure that the hospitality of the family culminated in the offer of a place to stay the night.' There follows her assessment of Dr and Mrs Haufe: 'both persons are marked by a bourgeois lifestyle . . . I would judge that they get their information from FRG [West German] mass media.' However, she does emphasize that they are not hostile to 'our social system'. Finally, she stresses the need to protect the source (that is, her) because 'only our two families know of the Englishman's visit'. In sending a copy of this report to Berlin, Lieutenant-Colonel Maresch, head of counter-intelligence in the Erfurt office, notes that the Haufes are now being investigated by his unit.

A month later, 'Michaela' reports on a further visit I paid to them. Here I apparently failed to recognize Dr Georg's daughter from his first marriage, whom I had met while visiting his first wife, the former Mrs Philby. 'Michaela' says that I then became very embarrassed and failed to explain convincingly whether I was really interested in Jewish resistance to Nazism or in Kim Philby. (The answer was: both.) She had also learned from Mrs Haufe that I had again visited them and gone for a walk in the Goethe cemetery with their son Christoph, who was studying in Jena. At the bottom of the page, Lieutenant Küntzel notes further measures to be taken. These include instructing 'Michaela' to develop the contact with me and further investigation of Christoph Haufe in Jena. For him, a student from an already suspect family, this could have had serious consequences. In that system, a few more black marks from the Stasi could add up to dismissal from the university. So here is a case where 'Michaela's' harmless prattle endangered someone who was vulnerable and could not simply move on, as I could. Yet the danger came, ultimately, from me.

Another month passes and this time 'Michaela' reports the text of a postcard which I had sent her, giving my telephone numbers in East and West Berlin. Measures to be taken include asking the ministry in Berlin to check the telephone numbers. When department II/9 replies saying the IM must have misread the numbers, the Erfurt office sends back a photocopy of the actual postcard, observing haughtily: 'The information given by our IM is thereby confirmed.' Signed 'pp. Lieutenant-Colonel Maresch'. This absurd bureaucratic rigmarole takes two months, from June to August, during which I had, in fact, virtually finished collecting the material for my book and left for Italy to start writing.

FIFTEEN YEARS ON, I now send copies of these documents to the Haufes, explaining that I hope to write about this file, that I would like to visit them again in Weimar and to ask 'Michaela' – if she is still there – why she did it and what she has to say for herself. Of course I appreciate that they may be quite unsympathetic to the whole undertaking. But the friendly dedication in my copy of Jochmann's *The Untimely Truth* leads me to hope that my visit in 1980 was not as unwelcome as it appears from the Stasi file.

When I telephone some time later, from Königswinter on the Rhine, Dr Haufe says they will be delighted to see me. I hire a car and drive to Weimar. The Haufes greet me in the Cranachstrasse with all the warmth I remember from fifteen years before. They assure me that my visit then had not been unwelcome. 'We were trying to remember,' says the energetic Frau Haufe. 'It was actually Christoph's birthday on the 25th. We had laid the table, with candles. Then you stood before the door. I took you into this room, I remember, I sat you down next to that table over there and brought you some food.' The Proustian effect again. 'You were somewhat reserved but certainly not pushy as *she* describes you.'

We talk for a while about the whole business of the files and dealing with the communist legacy. They remind me that the local State Security headquarters were at the far end of this same street. So Weimar was again home to the two extremes: Dr Haufe at this end of the Cranachstrasse, right next to the

Goethe and Schiller cemetery, the Stasi at the other. The Stasi were housed in a handsome villa designed by Henry van der Velde, like the nearby Nietzsche Archive. The Haufes' current files had apparently been destroyed before the building was occupied by local people – the Haufes among them – on 5 December 1989. But the Gauck Authority had found an earlier file on his expulsion from Leipzig University in 1957–8, the end of his academic career.

He had been denounced by, amongst others, one Dr Warmbier, a lecturer in Marxism-Leninism. Finding the address in the Leipzig phone book – there are not many Warmbiers in the Leipzig phone book – Dr Haufe sent him copies of the relevant pages. Dr Warmbier wrote back, apologized, but enclosed copies of pages from his own file showing how he had himself been sacked from the university in 1974 for his increasingly critical views and had then actually been sentenced to two years in prison for 'anti-state agitation'. Now Dr Warmbier had applied for rehabilitation and, says Eberhard Haufe, 'I would not like to be the person who has to judge that case'.

But what of 'Michaela'? Well, says Frau Haufe, theirs was never a close friendship. The friendship was really with Dr Georg, who had one day appeared with his daughter in tow saying, 'You have been recommended to us as a paediatrician'. But now she thinks the Stasi probably sent him. He was interesting, clever, witty. They had last seen him when he came to congratulate Dr Haufe on his fiftieth birthday in 1981. Meat was then scarce, but there was a butcher who made nice little platters of cold meats and he had brought one of those.

She, by contrast, was vulgar and selfish. And, says Frau Haufe, in high dudgeon and broad Thuringian, she has the cheek to tell the Stasi that we have a 'bourgeois lifestyle'! Here I was, getting up at six in the morning to clean the flat before going off to work, and there she was, lah-dih-dahing around in her

Schloss, employing a cleaning lady, which was very unusual in those days, yet she tells them *we* have a bourgeois lifestyle . . .

As a senior state employee, 'Michaela' was certainly obliged to cooperate with the Stasi, but she did not have to be an IM. Why did she do it? Probably for her career. She went on, after her husband's death, to work in the state art-dealing business in Berlin. This was closely involved with the notorious Stasi Colonel Alexander Schalck-Golodkowski, entrusted with obtaining as much hard currency as possible for the heavily indebted communist state, by hook or by crook. The Haufes have had no further contact with her, but perhaps she will be in the Berlin phone book . . .

AS I RACE UP the battered autobahn to Berlin, just as I used to all those years ago, I think back over this conversation: how a file opens the door to a vast sunken labyrinth of the forgotten past, but how, too, the very act of opening the door itself changes the buried artefacts, like an archaeologist letting in fresh air to a sealed Egyptian tomb.

For these are not simply past experiences rediscovered in their original state. Even without the fresh light from a new document or another's recollection – the opened door – our memories decay or sharpen, mellow or sour, with the passage of time and the change of circumstances. Thus Frau Haufe, for example, surely had a somewhat different memory of 'Michaela' in 1985, when the GDR still existed, than she did ten years later, on the eve of my visit. But with fresh light the memory changes irrevocably. A door opens, but another closes. There is no way back now to your own earlier memory of that person, that event. It is like a revelation made, years later, to a loved one. Or a bad divorce, where today's bitterness transforms all the shared past, completely, miserably, seemingly for ever. Except that this bitter memory, too, will fade and change with the further passage of time.

So what we have is nothing less than an infinity of memories of any moment, event or person: memories that change slowly, always, with every passing second, but now and then dramatically, after some jolt or revelation. Like one of those digital photographs whose every colour, tint or detail can be changed on a computer screen, except that here we're not in control and can't revert at will to an earlier image. They say 'the past is a foreign country', but actually the past is another universe.

Is it then ultimately true that, as Thomas Hobbes writes in a passage which James Fenton chose for the epigraph of his German Requiem, '*Imagination* and *Memory* are but one thing'? The Polish-American-Jewish writer Jerzy Kosinski used to let it be understood that, as a Jewish boy in Poland during the war, he was separated from his family, thrown into a slurry pit by the peasants in the village where he was hiding and perhaps even struck dumb at the age of nine, like the character in his novel *The Painted Bird*. The novel was promoted, praised and sold as a Holocaust testament. But researchers went to the village and found the surviving peasants there remembered it quite differently: the young Kosinski was never thrown into the slurry pit and anyway he had been hiding together with his family. Now either all the peasants' memories were wrong, or Kosinski's memory merged with imagination and he really believed these things had happened to him, or he deliberately embroidered his memories. His friends defended him fiercely. Erica Jong, for example, said, 'What difference does it make whether he experienced [these things] or not?'

Yet there is a real dividing-line between the memory, however faded or enriched, of something that actually happened, and imagining something that never happened. There are historical facts. Either the young Kosinski went splash into the slurry pit, or he did not. Either 'Michaela' signed a written undertaking to be a Stasi informer, or she did not.

Like the materials used in a collage, these pieces of evidence have very different textures: here a fragment of hard metal, there a scrap of faded newspaper, there again a wisp of cotton-wool. Reporters, investigators and historians will compose widely varying collages from the same box of scraps, and further change the picture with the oil-paints or water-colours of their own imagination. But there are special truth-tests to which their pictures, unlike the poet's or novelist's, must always submit. These tests will apply to every line I write. That is what makes it so difficult.

CHECKING IN TO A HOTEL, I reach for the phone book. There is one entry with 'Michaela's' real name. For a moment I wonder whether I should simply appear at her front door – in effect to 'doorstep' her, like a tabloid journalist from the *Sun* or *Bild-Zeitung* – or to risk failure by being a gentleman and phoning beforehand. I dial the number. 'Ah, Herr Esch, you visited us in Weimar didn't you, and I've since read your book . . .' I explain that I am very briefly in Berlin and have a particular reason for wanting to see her. We fix a time in the afternoon for me to call. 'You'll certainly have many questions', she says, and 'really I'm looking forward to it.'

A grey tower-block of characteristic socialist-modernist design, well-located and smart by East German standards. Privileged. A tall, rather loud woman greets me: 'Hello, how are you?' Large features, bright lipstick, grey eyes behind metallic spectacles. Trousers and high heels. A reach-me-down Marlene. Tasteful interior decor, neo-Biedermeier furniture.

'Well,' she says brightly, when we are settled with coffee and cakes, 'what are you up to these days?'

'Frau [real name],' I say, 'do you have an inkling of why I have sought you out today?'

A pause, just slightly too long, then: 'No, not really.' That 'really' again.

Then I tell her.

'Yes,' she says immediately, 'one was obliged to in my

position.' About once a month they would come to see her. Her secretary would say 'Boss, you have a visitor again'. They introduced themselves as coming from the local council, but gave only a first name: 'Heinz' or 'Dieter' or 'Michael'. The conversation was purely in her official capacity, *dienstlich, nur dienstlich*. But surely my visit was an entirely private one? Yes, but Litzi and Georg were convinced that I was working for British intelligence, so this was at least a semi-official matter, *halb-dienstlich*. How she clings to the sheet-anchor of *dienstlich*.

She talks in a rather matter-of-fact, outwardly self-confident way, but then asks, nervously: 'What did they report?' Not 'I' but 'they'.

I give her photocopies of the reports and she starts reading. She is shaken by the detail and by the information on her husband.

I ask how the interview normally proceeded. Did 'Dieter' or 'Heinz' have a notebook? Yes, yes, they had an open notebook and they carefully wrote everything down. And really one cooperated. One was obliged to. And one tried to tell as many harmless details as possible. And then, one thought they might help with one's work. And sometimes they did help: with difficulties over planning permission, things like that. The Stasi intervened, to get things done. And you see there was this law case about two Dürer pictures from the Weimar collection which American soldiers had stolen at the end of the war. And she thought: if we win the law suit, then perhaps I'll be sent to America to collect them! Well, they won, but the Ministry of Culture sent someone else to America. She complained to the Stasi about that.

Anyway, Dr Georg died in 1984, after his daughter by his first marriage to Litzi Philby had emigrated. On his death-bed he said he still believed in socialism. Then Litzi emigrated to Vienna, to be nearer to their daughter, 'Michaela's' step-daughter, who had recently been allowed out. Yes, Litzi had worked for the KGB; but by the end she was disillusioned and resolutely apolitical. Then 'Michaela's' own daughter, her child by Dr Georg, had emigrated. She herself moved to Berlin, took early retirement – with a good pension as the widow of a 'fighter against fascism' – and, in 1987, resigned from the Party. In a friend's file there had been mention of contacts with 'the Jew [Dr Georg's real name]'. That was shocking, although of course one knew there was this latent anti-semitism around. 'But I haven't applied to see my own file, I don't want to do that.' She seems half-way to seeing herself as an object of Stasi surveillance, almost as a dissident.

But then she goes back to reading the photocopies. The banal, grotesque detail she had supplied about me, about the Haufes and their 'bourgeois lifestyle', about young Christoph Haufe. Lieutenant Küntzel's list of measures to be taken: investigation of the family and of the student Christoph, instructing the IM for a further contact. Suddenly she puts the papers down and says, 'I can't read any more. I feel sick, I want to puke'. She turns and walks to the door, and when she comes back she is crying. Her voice is strangled as she says, 'This can't be excused'. Still, she tries to explain.

Her grandfather was a Prussian officer, but her grandmother was Jewish. So according to the Nazi classification in the Nuremberg Laws her father was a so-called *Mischling*. However, because he was a gifted gynaecologist the SS employed him, despite his mixed blood, in one of their own maternity hospitals in Thuringia. After the war, her father had come back to be a senior doctor in Brandenburg, joining first the Social Democrats and then the Socialist Unity Party formed from the forced merger of the Social Democrats with the Communists. She was fifteen in 1945, and for her this was a time of elation and true belief in a new beginning. She was sure they were building a better Germany. Of course, she says, the style of the new regime was awfully petit-bourgeois and philistine for someone from her background, but still. Her hopes faded only slowly. The Soviet crushing of the Prague Spring was an important moment of disillusionment. But even in the 1970s she still believed that socialism was the better system. Anyway, it was there, it was the only thing she had known all her adult life.

In 1975 she got this good job in Weimar. But with it came 'Dieter' and 'Heinz'. As she talks, emotionally, disjointedly, she reveals rather vividly the mixture of motives that made her collaborate. Some residual belief in the system. The sense that it was an official duty: 'in that position one was obliged to . . .' Then there was the hope of using the Stasi as a player in the bureaucratic game. For her own purposes too: through Dürer to America! Also, Georg and Litzi thought I really was a spy and, after all, there was a war on, wasn't there? A cold war between her system and mine.

And fear?

'Yes, of course, underneath one was shit-scared of them.' So one tried to disarm any suspicion, to show how cooperative one was, by chatting away, giving all sorts of harmless detail. 'And this is what comes out . . .'

As she looks at the photocopied reports of IM 'Michaela' she nearly breaks down again, the eyes behind the metallic spectacles filling with tears.

'Really one should write to the Haufes.' She struggles to regain her composure, wrestling with what she has done.

'But this wasn't responsible for your being banned, was it?'

No, that followed the publication of my book in West Germany.

Ah, that was just like them. It was always the *West's* opinion that really mattered to them. 'That should have made me think.'

'And now you want to write something? And you wanted to see

my reaction? And now I've reacted like this and that's good for you, isn't it?' She laughs bitterly, then asks: 'Will you name names?'

I explain that I do not want to hurt anyone and will not use her real name. However, because of the Weimar and Philby connections it will be very difficult to tell the story without her being identifiable, to family and acquaintances at least.

She is buffeted by conflicting thoughts and emotions. One moment she says, 'Really it's good that you've shown me this'. The next: 'Ah well, perhaps I can sue you and I'll win a lot of money . . . No, no, sorry, that was only a joke . . . But perhaps there is some protection . . .'

'We repressed so much . . . *Why* didn't I apply to see my file? Because I didn't want to know what was in it . . . and about my husband . . . Who knows what else there is . . . I think this was the only time I reported so extensively on private matters. I thought it was *dienstlich* but . . . Well, I hope if you do write you'll try to explain the subjective as well as the objective conditions. How it was then. But probably that's impossible. Even I can't really remember now . . .'

The conversation dies in the twilight. What can I say at parting? 'It was a pleasure to see you again'? Hardly. Or: 'I'm sorry to have done this to you'? I say: 'The copies are for you. Please write to me if you have anything you want to add. Here is my address.'

And she replies: 'Ah, Oxford!' She had spent a lovely day there recently. She goes to England every year, to visit old friends. Childhood friends of Litzi. 'Have you written down your telephone number? Perhaps next time I'll ring you up!'

As we shake hands at the front door, she does not say 'sorry'. She says: 'How did you get here, by car?'

No, by underground.

'Oh, it's a very good connection isn't it?' Struggling for self-respect and normality, as if nothing had happened. Nothing really.

When I sit down in my hotel room half-an-hour later and take out a pen, I find that my own hand is trembling.

YOU MUST IMAGINE conversations like this taking place every evening, in kitchens and sitting-rooms all over Germany. Painful encounters, truth-telling, friendship-demolishing, life-haunting. Hundreds, thousands of such encounters, as the awful power of knowledge is slowly passed down from the Stasi to the employees of the Gauck Authority, and from the employees of the Gauck Authority to individuals like me. Who then hold the lives of other people in our hands, in a way that most of us would never otherwise do.

Might it not, after all, be wiser to allow them their own particular imaginative mixture of memory and forgetting, of self-respect built on self-deception? Or is it better to confront them? Better not just for yourself, for your own need to know, but for them too? Even in her first confused reaction, 'Michaela' herself said 'really it's good that you've shown me this'.

When we talked, she strongly denied knowing that the Stasi had her down as an informer. At first I was inclined to believe her, but experts and friends told me not to be so naive: 'That's what they always say.' Frau Duncker, who has taken over my case on Frau Schulz's retirement, now suggests that the archive might trace 'Michaela's' own file. As a normal reader, you are only given photocopies of the pages from the informer's file that relate directly to you. You can also request formal, written confirmation of the real identity of those who informed on you, 'insofar as this is clearly established by the documents'. As a researcher I am, exceptionally, allowed to see their actual files.

A regular informer's file has three parts, compiled according to strict rules. Part I documents the biography of the informer, the way in which the Stasi has won their cooperation, up to and including the written pledge to work as an informer, with personal choice of code-name, and their subsequent record, including photocopies of their private correspondence, information given on them by other informers and a note of any concerns the Stasi has about their reliability. Part II contains their work: detailed notes by their Stasi case officer on the information they give at regular meetings, usually in 'conspiratorial flats', their own written reports, reviews of the year's work, plans for further action and so on. Part III has receipts for all the expenses and 'premiums' paid to them.

Unfortunately, the archive can only find Part II of 'Michaela's' file, and not all of that. Still, it is big enough to be going on with: nearly six hundred pages, covering the period 1976 to 1984. The Weimar years. It begins with Lieutenant Küntzel reassuring 'Michaela' that, as he puts its, 'our organ' will ensure that there will be no unfortunate consequences for her because she was caught taking hard currency out of the country illegally during an official trip to Hungary. 'Michaela' is very relieved about this. She had feared repercussions for her future official trips abroad. A few weeks later he visits her again, and records that she expressed readiness to work 'with our organ ... in respect of her professional concerns. She feels herself personally unsuited for other tasks.' Her husband had told her a little about what *that* was like. He had known Kim Philby well 'and also worked for the friends during his time in exile in England'. ('The friends' is a phrase people in East Germany used, often ironically, to refer to the Russians.) 'She did not feel herself to be suited to such work.'

Two months later she can report on a successful official trip to Switzerland: something of which most East Germans could only dream. Lieutenant Küntzel confirms with her his 'legend', that he comes from the district council. And here already I find the first handwritten report, signed 'Michaela'.

One has to be careful, though. Later in the file there are other handwritten reports, also signed 'Michaela', but these are in the handwriting of the person who took over from Lieutenant Küntzel the conduct of regular meetings with her. (This man – was it 'Dieter' or 'Heinz'? – was not a regular officer at all, but an informer whose job was to run other informers.) In the earlier reports, however, the large female hand does appear to be that of 'Michaela' herself. In fact, one document in this handwriting – a draft letter to the cultural attachés at several embassies – is signed with her real name, which has then been crossed out and 'Michaela' written over it.

Her second handwritten report concerns a matter of huge importance for the security of the state. Across three pages, 'Michaela' complains about the service in the restaurant of the Hotel Elephant. She has been most rudely treated by the head waiter, Herr Göbbel, in front of her English guests, who made fun of this. 'Above all,' she writes, 'the dictatorial tone [of Herr Göbbel] was described as unworthy of an international hotel. This sort of guest care does not, in my opinion, enhance the international reputation of the GDR.'

On 15 September 1976, Lieutenant Küntzel notes that their next appointment, on 21 September, will be the interview to recruit her formally as an informer. The meeting will take place, unusually, in her own flat. The record of that crucial conversation is not in this binder, presumably because it was placed, following the standard procedures, in Part I of her file, together with any handwritten pledge – if pledge there was. However, she is subsequently designated with the abbreviation for an informer having direct contact with the enemy, IMV. Later in the file she is described as IMS, the abbreviation for an informer on the security of a particular area. And she certainly kept talking.

That autumn, for example, there is a prominent West German visitor to the Art Galleries, one Helmut Kohl. 'Michaela' deplores the fact that, encouraged by Comrade [name], the attendants had been overzealous in their duties, 'opening doors and making bows'.

What follows is less amusing. At meetings every two or three weeks, a pattern interrupted only by her holidays and official trips abroad, she gives generously of her time and knowledge. She reports on the political attitudes of her subordinates: this one had criticized the expulsion of the dissident singer Wolf Biermann, that one showed 'an almost bourgeois attitude to various problems of our society'. She supplies a five-page hand-written report on a visit to someone she describes as one of her best friends in the West.

Reading such a file you see how an informer is gradually played in, like a fish on a line, starting from the initial resolve to talk only of 'professional concerns' and ending up with the most private betrayal. For in the end, 'Michaela' even informs on the West German boyfriend of her own step-daughter. Under 'Instructions to the IM on further measures', Lieutenant Küntzel then writes the chilling words '*Abschöpfung der Tochter*'. *Abschöpfung* is another Stasi technical term, laboriously defined in the 1985 Stasi dictionary as 'systematic conduct of conversations for the targeted exploitation of the knowledge, information and possibilities of other persons for gaining information'. The nearest English equivalent is, I suppose, 'pumping'. So 'Michaela' is to pump her step-daughter for the secret police.

Perhaps she really thought she was just chatting away to 'Dieter' or 'Heinz', showing that she was a good comrade and loyal citizen with nothing to hide. Harmless gossip you know.

Perhaps she never imagined that it would all be written down in such detail, although she seems – if my handwriting analysis is correct – to have been quite ready to write things down in detail herself. Certainly such 'instructions' may bear little relation to what actually happened, as I know from my own file. A friendly 'how's your step-daughter getting on these days?' becomes the chilling '*Abschöpfung der Tochter*'. But if she didn't know what she was doing, that's because she didn't want to know what she was doing.

To make a fair judgement, I would like to know precisely what damage, if any, was done to the people 'Michaela' talked about, but this is very difficult to establish. As required by the law, names of innocent third parties are blacked out. Even if I could still identify them, I would not be given access to their files. Only by looking at those records could I assess the effect of her information, as against that coming from other sources. Hence only those who were directly affected, and now choose to read their own files, can really say. Yet we do know that the Stasi paid particular attention to information coming from the IMs. Their seemingly harmless snippets of information were stitched together into something altogether more harmful. That was how the whole system worked.

Meanwhile, although I cannot definitely say what difficulties she caused others, I can say what benefit she derived for herself. A month later, for example, an internal memorandum confirms that there are no objections at all to her continuing to travel abroad: a rare privilege. After they discuss how she might serve the state on her forthcoming trip to Japan, Lieutenant Küntzel notes: 'The tasks assigned to the IM have always been readily accepted and realized. IMV "Michaela" has acquired operative knowledge and abilities which enable him[sic] to realize complicated tasks.' The 'him' refers to IM, *Inoffizielle Mitarbeiter*, for which the Stasi did not recognize the female form, *Mitarbeiterin*.

In fact, this was a largely masculine world: only some 10 per cent of Stasi informers were women.

In September 1979, I appear on the scene. At the next meeting, Lieutenant Küntzel 'instructs' her on how to behave towards me. A week later, I haven't been in touch. A month later, and still no word from me: 'The IM was concerned that he [i.e., she] might have done something wrong. These doubts could be allayed.' Summing up the year's work at the end of December, Lieutenant Küntzel notes with satisfaction that the IM was now ready to do things that [s]he was not ready to do at the outset. 'The main point was identified as the contact with Garton Ash. The IM was praised in respect of the [sic] behaviour.'

The reports for 1980 and 1981 follow our sporadic contacts, as recorded on my own file, interspersed with her trips to Italy and Denmark. In late 1981 the informer-for-running-informers, code-name 'Singer', takes over from the Lieutenant. 'Michaela' continues to sing for her exit visas. In March 1982, 'Singer' and 'Michaela' are recorded as 'evaluating' extracts from my book about East Germany which had appeared in *Der Spiegel*. In June, 'Singer' congratulates her on receiving the Fatherland Order of Merit in Silver, and adds a present of 50 marks from the Ministry. At the next meeting, she reports at length the saga of the Dürers. Unless I had talked to her, I would never have understood from reading this document that it was all about her frustration at being denied the chance to visit America.

And so it goes on, and on. A contact with the Swiss embassy. The assessment of another employee. A present from the Ministry for 'Michael' – that is, Dr Georg – on his eightieth birthday. 'A congenial gathering took place in dignified festive fashion', writes 'Singer'. Then a report on her step-daughter's new husband.

A trip to Austria. Dr Georg falls gravely ill. A meeting which 'served the purpose of showing "Michaela" that in the coming hard time she [for once, the female form is used] can find support from our organ'. Her report of a letter from Litzi, the former Mrs Philby, saying that she would not be returning to East Germany after a trip to Vienna.

Then Dr Georg's death, retirement from the Weimar job and the proposed move to Berlin, eased by a widow's letter to Politburo member Kurt Hager (alias Feliks Albin), who knew Dr Georg from their time in London during the war. But just before she goes: a last little report on an artist who had applied to emigrate . . .

AS I EXPLORE the trivial and sometimes intimate details of 'Michaela's' collaboration I stop to ask myself: should I really be reading all this? And even if I should, should you?

When writers or newspaper editors are criticized for publishing details from someone's private life, they cite 'the public interest'. But in practice their definition of 'public interest' is often 'what interests the public' – that is, what sells more of their newspapers or books. Is there, here, a genuine public interest to justify publishing personal details that will certainly embarass 'Michaela' and may even damage her relationship with her step-daughter?

A formal answer can be found in the law on the Stasi files. According to Article 32, for the purposes of the historical exploration of the Stasi's history and 'political education' I may see and publish personal information from the files on 'persons of contemporary history, holders of a political function or office-holders exercising their office, so long as they are not adversely affected persons or third parties'; on those who worked for the Stasi, whether full-time or as any of the various kinds of unofficial collaborator; and on those who benefited from the Stasi's work. However, this applies only so long as 'no overriding protection-worthy interests of such persons are adversely affected'.

But who is a 'person of contemporary history' and what is an 'overriding protection-worthy interest'? A legal expert at the Gauck Authority explains. The former are what in English would be called 'public figures'. However, German law makes a further distinction between 'absolute' and 'relative' historical figures. 'Absolute' historical figures are people like Hitler or Churchill. 'Relative' historical figures are people of historical importance only in a particular area or time, and just that part of their life is, so to speak, fair game. 'Protection-worthy interests' are sensitive details from the person's private life, inasmuch as these are not important to understanding how the Stasi worked.

In practice, the employees of the Gauck Authority have to make countless individual judgements as they prepare the files for the reader. As well as blacking out the names of 'affected and third parties' while leaving those of 'persons of contemporary history', they are to cover up passages which concern such 'protection-worthy interests'. Several pages on 'Michaela's' file are covered up for this reason.

For some time, I thought it was they who had to make the hard decisions and take the legal responsibility, but the expert puts me straight. I alone am answerable in court for what I publish. So 'Michaela' might, as she fantasized, sue me. But I am not worried about that. What concerns me is not the legal responsibility but the moral one. For example, why not simply leave out the bit about her step-daughter? Fortunately, I manage to locate the step-daughter, and carefully explain the position. She knows already that her stepmother had informed on her. She found out about it by reading her own file and as a result has severed all ties. 'Michaela's' own daughter also learned about it on that occasion.

This still leaves the woman herself and her relationships with other people. As I work on this book, I discuss the problem with friends. Some think I should spare 'Michaela'. 'Otherwise you become like her', they say. 'Now you're the informer.' Others think I should definitely publish, simply because it's *interesting*. That matters, of course, but in itself is not enough. What makes me decide to publish – although without naming names – is the conviction that this also serves a larger purpose. Here is a chance to bring home, with the vividness that can only come from such intimate detail, how someone is drawn into a secret police net – and to show where such collaboration will lead you.

VI

IM 'SCHULDT' SUPPLIES several minutely detailed reports of encounters at which we appear mainly to have discussed the history of the Third Reich. Except for his description of my room in Prenzlauer Berg, they do not add much. As 'Schuldt' himself ruefully observes of one meeting: 'All in all, this "working lunch" was not very successful for me.'

My diary enables me to identify him. He was a middle-aged lecturer in English Literature whom I had met, incongruously, at the Queen's Birthday Party in the garden of the British Ambassador's residence. I remember him as heavy-featured, balding, lugubrious and quite boring, though with good English and occasional drops of wit.

He seems to have been the kind of informer – the experts at the Gauck Authority tell me there were many such – who spent countless hours writing or typing absurdly detailed reports. The Stasi was their pen pal. The Pooterish depths this reached can be seen in an extract from the professor's account of a lunch with the Third Secretary at the British Embassy, included in my file because they also discussed me. 'The whole atmosphere of the meeting with Mr Wildash,' records IM 'Schuldt', 'was businesslike but more conventional than I had expected (is this a case of the conventional distance of a young man from a 'professor'?) While I was at pains to order Czech specialities (e.g., dumplings) to eat, my companion partook of a dish of chicken liver. He drank two or three bottles of Pils, although he had come by car.' I wonder how many miles of such stuff –

'(e.g., dumplings)' – there are in the one-hundred-and-eleven miles of files now administered by the Gauck Authority. Twenty miles? Forty?

'Schuldt's' own file helps me to understand why he did it. This time, the archivists find all three parts of an exemplary informer's record. His Part I comprises two substantial binders, Part II no fewer than four and even the slim Part III, documenting his expenses, is strangely eloquent. Together, they tell a sad story. It begins in 1960. 'Schuldt' is a bright but erratic junior lecturer in English at a provincial university. He is in his early thirties, unmarried, had attended a good school during the war and briefly been in the Hitler Youth. His head of department thinks he sometimes does not pay enough attention to detail, but finds his work full of stimulating ideas. His spoken English is clearly good, since he has recently returned from serving as a special interpreter on a trip to Asia with the prime minister.

But now he has been denounced for telling disrespectful anecdotes about this trip in a pub, for drinking too much and for making homosexual advances to students. A student reports one incident in detail. After many rounds of drinks, he had invited them back to his flat and started making advances: '["Schuldt"] then said that if [the student] took off his leather shorts he would fetch another bottle of wine from the cellar.' 'Schuldt' defends himself in a ten-page typewritten letter, full of references to the position of homosexuality in European cultural history and craven self-criticism. His conduct was, he writes, 'a grave violation of my duties as a member of the Party'. He will now 'endeavour to bear the title of Comrade with honour'.

There follow preliminary conversations with the 'Candidate'. The blackmail is not explicitly recorded, but there is a full account of the formal recruitment interview in the town hall on 29 December 1961, between 9 and 11.30 a.m. He gives detailed assessments of many colleagues in the university. Then there is a special brown envelope bound into the file. Printed on the cover is the single word 'Pledge' – the pledge, that is, to work for the Stasi. This envelope is empty. Part II, however, contains a full record of his work from 1962 onwards, with regular, detailed reports on colleagues, students and acquaintances. Meanwhile, Part I continues a watchful trickle of other informers' reports on him (in 1970 he's still drinking heavily) and photocopies of his correspondence. Part III records the expenses: 5 marks for food and drink, 28 marks for wine and cigars, 100 for telephone, 200 for travel, and the occasional 'premium' for good work.

In 1975 we find a certificate recording the presentation of a Bronze Medal for 'loyal service in the National People's Army'. This Medal is awarded, says the citation, 'as a sign of recognition for honest, conscientious and loyal duty done in the Ministry for State Security'. Signed by Erich Mielke, the Minister For State Security.

'Schuldt' now becomes more interesting to the Stasi because he meets the First Secretary at the British Embassy. He energetically pursues this friendly contact, in close coordination with his case officer. Included are photocopies of the title pages of several volumes of the *Penguin Modern Poets* sent him by the genial First Secretary, as also are copies of all their correspondence. In the third volume we find him enjoying the privilege of attending a conference on English literature at Peterhouse College, Cambridge. Detailed assessments of several of the participants follow. Professor Raymond Williams is singled out as a 'progressive citizen'.

In volume four I appear – drinking, as he sourly notes, rather a lot of his brandy. Perhaps he hopes for a refill from the Stasi. (According to the expenses chits, at their next meeting his case officer gives him 200 marks, ostensibly for the costs of a trip to Berlin but enough to cover several bottles.) He then submits his own memorandum on another possible visit to England. There is a dinner at the British Ambassador's residence in the spring of 1980, with George Steiner as the guest of honour ('Professor Steiner continued to hold forth . . .'), and another in the autumn, to which, he carefully reports, Timothy Garton Ash was given a lift by Mark Wood of Reuters. In December 1980 he receives a premium of 300 marks and is praised especially for his work on the British Embassy, all done, the commendation notes, 'in his free time'. Then, in January 1981, they develop a strategy for trying to restore the contact with me.

At the same time, however, department 26 is bugging his flat, and they record him saying to a friend: 'the GDR keeps collapsing'. So he's unlikely to be getting a Silver Medal. But the meetings, the reports and the little presents continue. In March 1984, he suggests that he might go to Poland to re-establish contact with that British diplomat, now at the Embassy in Warsaw. Always game for a little trip at the Stasi's expense. But there the volume abruptly ends.

I turn back to Part I and find, folded inside another brown envelope, a 'concluding report' dated 4 October 1984. 'The last meeting with IM "Schuldt" took place on 16.5.84', it says. 'On 10.7.84 IM "Schuldt" died unexpectedly.' He was fifty-seven. 'No political-operative consequences follow from the sudden demise of IM "Schuldt".'

VII

IMB 'SMITH' CONTRIBUTES a sartorial criticism. He says I 'make a pretty casual impression (open collar, which requires a tie, but no tie...)'.

He places me, accurately enough, as 'a member of the bourgeois intelligentsia with a liberal-humanist education and a liberal-democratic attitude'. He also finds me 'somewhat naive in [my] curiosity. Seeks every opportunity to learn more. Talks to old workers in "the pub at the corner", that is, with citizens who remember [the Nazi] period.'

I cannot remember 'Smith' at all, and my diary notes only 'long lunch w. British Communist at Humboldt Univ.' After several false traces – are there so many 'Smiths'? – the archivists finally bring up the right file. He is an Englishman, a former polytechnic lecturer who took a job teaching at the Humboldt University in the 1970s, married an East German woman and settled down. Here, in Part I of the file, is Lieutenant Wendt's proposal to make contact with him, using a 'legend'. Wendt will ring up, pretending to be from the city council. When they meet, Wendt will introduce himself as 'Heinz Lenz' from the Ministry for State Security and say that the Englishman's name has appeared on the books of a Western intelligence service in West Berlin. It looks bad, and they need his cooperation to clear this up. In effect: prove your innocence!

The trick works. Within a week, there's another meeting with candidate-informer 'Doktor', as he's now called. Two weeks later, the candidate writes out and signs a handwritten undertaking to keep these contacts strictly secret. Later in Part I, I find the standard brown envelope saying 'Pledge'. It contains his handwritten pledge to 'support the M[inistry] f[or] S[tate Security] on a voluntary basis'. For this purpose, it concludes, 'I have chosen the code-name "Smith"'. By 1981, he's an IMB. This abbreviation replaced IMV (as for 'Michaela') in 1980, but meant essentially the same: the highest class of informer, one having direct contact with the enemy.

As an Englishman, you always think to yourself: if Britain had a communist police state, would we have lots of informers? Well, here's a British informer – and a busy one. His Part II comprises some 600 pages, in three binders, and that takes us only to 1986. The last binder cannot be found; perhaps it was still in Wendt's office cupboard, perhaps it was shredded or burned.

He starts by informing mainly on his contacts with the British Embassy. Then he is asked to report on the British Council library in West Berlin. A detailed description – with sketch map – is delivered. Then there are formal typewritten instructions for a trip to Britain. What to do if the British 'special services' try to contact him: 'Don't become nervous, remain outwardly calm!' His special mission is to give a detailed description – with sketch map – of the British Council headquarters in Spring Gardens, in central London. Leave it to 'Smith'. And sure enough, here is his biro sketch map: Whitehall, Trafalgar Square, the Mall and then Spring Gardens drawn in the wrong place.

Later, he is given another formal instruction. From 11.00 hrs to 13.00 hrs on 4 December 1982 he is to observe a female person and her partner in the Jade restaurant at the Europa-Center in West Berlin. For this, he will receive DM150 expenses. His report, which is far from illuminating, says he suspects that the Chinese waiter was watching them too.

Between these more or less farcical missions comes the handwritten version of his encounter with me and fairly detailed information on other British people in East Germany. Then, to execute the plan of action at the beginning of my file – 'taking account of the subjective and objective possibilities of the IM' – there are minutely detailed instructions for the attempt to re-establish contact with me. He should try to find out from Mr Wildash at the British Embassy where I am, but do so casually. 'Not a lecture!' cautions Wendt. 'Smith', like many academics, is clearly inclined to lecture instead of converse. They agree the text of a letter which he is to ask Wildash to forward to me. And here is the letter. Perhaps I may remember our meeting? He has now read my articles on Poland and would like to discuss them further:

> If you are in Berlin at any time (West or East), I would be
> glad of a chance to meet and chat about these things. If you
> have produced more material and could send copies of it,
> that would also be very welcome (in this event, I need hardly
> add, please send it to the British Embassy with a note inside
> saying who it is for, and not to my private address!)

I like that 'I need hardly add': for fear of the Stasi, you know.

I have no recollection of ever receiving this letter but now, fifteen years later, it is delivered to me in a file.

By 1986, the department seems to be fed up with 'Smith' giving them long-winded lectures on European politics instead of what he is meant to deliver, the dirt on people. I begin to see what the Lieutenant meant about the limited 'subjective possibilities' of Professor 'Smith'. But then, in mid-1986, the record abruptly stops.

He's in the phone book, too. Hello, I say, perhaps you may remember our meeting?

'Yes, vaguely.'

Lunch?

'Fine.'

Could an Englishman look exactly like an East German man on the street? Leave it to 'Smith'. Anorak, brown trousers, white socks and brown shoes. (Even Lieutenant Wendt is moved to comment on the file that 'Smith' is 'neatly but not fashionably dressed'.) He has a pink, freckled face and a nervous smile.

Would he like the chicken?

Yes, he says, 'ta'.

Now I tell him. I am reading my file. An IM 'Smith' informed on me. It appears that 'Smith' was him.

'It's possible,' he says.

Then, without any further prompting, he gives his own account of the original approach, starting with the first telephone call from the 'city council'. He was very worried. He thought it was an approach from the CIA. Then they met, as arranged, in front of the Humboldt University, found an empty lecture room inside and 'Heinz Lenz' showed his State Security pass. He was shocked; still more so when 'Heinz Lenz' explained that they suspected him of being caught up with a Western secret service. He says 'Lenz' laid it on pretty thick, 'in James Bondish terms'. By the time 'Lenz' had finished with him, he was in a state of panic. He was terrified that they would expel him – and then what would happen to his wife and child, trapped behind the Wall? He went home and discussed it with his wife. They decided that he should cooperate, to prove that he was trustworthy.

The wrong decision, of course, but completely understandable. However, he goes on to explain that he also thought of the Stasi as a channel of communication to the state. In a small way, he says, he was trying to do what the leading church official Manfred Stolpe – down in the files as IM 'Secretary' but now

Social Democrat Prime Minister of Brandenburg – had been trying to do through his contacts with the Stasi: to get a political message to the top. The trouble with a communist state like East Germany was that it had 'no civil society framework'. He was making up for that lack.

He thought then that the Stasi was a small backroom outfit, 'something like MI5'. Only since 1989 has he realized what a huge empire it was. He has followed the debate in the press and finds it 'incredible' what some people did: spying on their friends, helping to 'put them in jug'.

His own 'principle' was to talk to the Stasi about social and political issues, but not about people. He would like, nonetheless, to know how far he 'adhered to it'. This seems the right moment to show him a copy of what he wrote about me. He is flustered as he reads and avoids my gaze for some moments afterwards. Says he's 'irritated' by it. 'Contrite, to put it mildly.'

He had wondered lately if it was true what they told him, about his being found on the books of 'a Western intelligence service'. Why didn't they say which service? He absolutely believed it at the time, but now he thinks the chances are '40:60' that they invented it.

I tell him they did.

Then I ask about the episode in the Jade restaurant. Was it exciting? Did he see himself as James Bond?

No, he was terrified. He thought he would get shot! Afterwards, he asked them never to send him on a mission like that again. Still, at least he could spend the Deutschmarks on Western books and newspapers.

And the sketch maps of the British Council?

Embarrassment again. He thought that was just 'a little test'.

He and the officers – there were several of them over the years – spoke much as we are speaking now. Why, then, did he make such copious handwritten notes? 'Because I've a bad memory.' He would speak from the notes, then hand them over. The officers were a strange mixture of formality and informality. After some time, 'Heinz Lenz' told him the Ministry had concluded he was not a Western spy and that, as a mark of trust, 'we would like to suggest saying *Du*'. Call me Heinz, and keep talking.

As for the information he supplied on individual people, he really thought these were innocent little fragments. What was important to him was the general political analysis, which he gave them at length. I point out that what was important to him was not to them. It was precisely those tiny fragments they were interested in. Afterwards they put them together, like archaeologists reconstructing a Roman pot. Yes, he sees that now.

At the end of lunch he asks nervously 'will you use my name?' He'd rather I didn't.

I say I will not. I'll leave it as 'Smith'.

A few months later, I deliver a public lecture in Berlin on what to do about the communist past. I discuss in some detail the opening of the Stasi files, including my own experience. Among the people who come up to me afterwards I am surprised to see 'Smith'. He gives me an envelope. Opening it back at my hotel, I find a letter saying that he has applied to see his file and that he would be glad to meet again 'to consider individual points'.

Meanwhile, he attaches a three-page typescript entitled, *Some thoughts on the MfS*. This makes no mention at all of his own involvement but discusses the whole problem in general terms, as one interested scholar writing to another. For example: 'The material in MfS files reflects the self-image of the MfS (manner of reporting, interpretation, terminology etc.) Anyone conversant with text analysis and the problems of perception and objectives in creating texts will appreciate the care that is needed in interpreting material of this kind.'

The word 'I' does not appear once in his text.

VIII

I FIRST MET FRAU R. at a small exhibition about the anti-fascist resistance in Berlin. A white-haired lady in her sixties, she immediately stood out from those around her by her bearing and style, poised, well-dressed, well-spoken. In fact, she came from a wealthy and cultured German Jewish family. She had converted to communism as a teenage girl in the early 1930s and, soon after Hitler came to power, was expelled from school as a result. She left Germany, met a partner for life and followed him to Moscow. They married and had a son. Soon, like so many others, he was arrested in one of the Stalinist purges and spent more than ten years in Soviet camps. She herself had to serve in one of the so-called 'labour armies'; for a time, her son was taken from her and put into an orphanage.

Many years later, in the mid-1950s, they managed to return to what was now the communist part of Germany. They had another child. Her husband never fully recovered from his years in the camps but here she at least had a good job, like-minded friends and her precious children. But then, shortly before the frontier to West Germany was finally sealed by the building of the Wall, her first-born fled to the West with his wife and small child. She did not see them again for ten years.

With these personal tragedies all flowing directly from communist rule, you might think she would have become a violent anti-communist. But with a quiet, melancholy passion she declared herself still convinced of the ultimate rightness and greatness of the communist cause. Was this to make sense of her suffering? If the cause was just and great, then all had not been in vain. She had suffered today so that others might know a better tomorrow. But that was only my guess.

In conversation, she indulged no pathos. Instead, she was full of curiosity, anecdote and sharp judgements, delivered in a quick, business-like, nasal voice. We got on famously. My diary records an enjoyable supper at her quiet flat, with its parquet floors and overflowing wooden bookshelves. Then there was a chance meeting at the East German premiere of Rolf Hochhuth's play *Lawyers*, which dealt with the scandal of a former Nazi military judge who, after sending people to their deaths, often for trivial offences, had gone on to hold high office in West Germany.

On 15 April 1980, I find, we went to see *The Peasants*, a play by East Germany's leading post-Brechtian dramatist, Heiner Müller, and then returned to her flat for what my diary calls a 'heart-to-heart'. The diary records her saying to me: 'Ah, if you were my son. How well your parents must have brought you up.' I wondered then what my parents would have made of this tribute from a German-Jewish communist. I sympathized with her, admired her, thought of her as a friend.

So I am really saddened when Frau Schulz hands me pages from a file identifying her as an informer for an operational group of Main Department XX, which was responsible, among other things, for penetrating and overseeing cultural life, the universities, the churches and what they called 'political underground activity'. The first report brings another surprise. It says the playwright Rolf Hochhuth, whom I had earlier met and talked to about his work, had told her that he regarded me as a British spy. 'The further deployment of the IM,' it concludes, 'is to some extent possible'.

'As per instructions,' begins the next report, dated 28 April

1980, 'the contact of an IM of HA XX/OG to the English citizen Gardon-Ash, Timothi, was developed.' There follows information on our visit to the Heiner Müller play and our subsequent conversation about my work on the resistance to Nazism. 'To the comment of the IM that such work was overdue in Britain, and to the arguments that the GDR had historically overcome this past – by contrast with the FRG [i.e., West Germany] – Gardon-Ash reacted negatively. He denied the existence of fascist tendencies in the FRG and emphasized that he has many good friends there.

'Gardon-Ash seemed to be most impressed by Weimar. He would shortly be going there again, to take part in the Shakespeare conference.

'The IM once again alluded to the comment made by Rolf Hochmuth [sic], who had described Gardon-Ash as a British spy, to which G. replied that Hochmuth, like so many others, reads too many unserious newspapers, according to which every second Englishman abroad must be a spy. He did not get embarrassed.'

A third report gives an account, from the same file, of another meeting I had with survivors of the communist resistance to Nazism in Berlin. Whether this is actually a report from Frau R. or from another member of the group is not entirely clear. Asked why I was working on this subject, I apparently replied that Oxford and Cambridge traditionally assign such topics. 'A hint by the source [i.e., the Stasi's informer] that in the twenties and thirties many friends of communism came from these universities (Kim Philby) was met by Gorton-Ash with wordless irony.'

Fifteen years on, I again sit on the same sofa, in the same flat, but with rather different feelings. Frau R. is very old now, but still *soignée* and sharp. When I tell her why I have come to see her again, she says: 'So what should I do? Jump out of the window?' She flatly denies knowing that the Stasi had her down as an informer and simply refuses to look at the photocopies I have brought with me from the file.

Then she reminds me of her great sufferings under the communism in which she so long believed. 'No, Tim,' she says, 'it's all not so simple.' And as she talks – with pathos now – of the horrors of the camps, of her dead husband, of her faraway son, we both understand that she is placing the weight of her suffering into the scales of my judgement. The weight is heavy. Within minutes I am telling her that I have no right to sit here as her judge. Her secret will be safe with me. She should, please, live her last years in peace and contentment.

But as I leave I can see, in her eyes, that this will haunt her. Not, I think, because of the mere fact of collaboration – she was, after all, a communist in a communist state – but because working with the secret police, being down in the files as an informer, is low and mean. All this is such a far, far cry from the high ideals of that brave and proud Jewish girl who set out, a whole lifetime ago, to fight for a better world. And, of course, there will still be the lingering fear of exposure, if not through me then perhaps through someone else.

I now almost wish I had never confronted her. By what right, for what good purpose, did I deny an old lady, who had suffered so much, the grace of selective forgetting?

IX

FROM THE AUTUMN OF 1980, the file is full of Poland. An internal memo notes that I again plan to travel there. How did they know? There is a detailed report of my conversation about 'the counter-revolutionary organization KSS "KOR"' with an editor of an 'anti-Soviet émigré journal' in Bonn. Did they tap my phone or his? On the same sheet, there is information from another source that 'because of the situation in Poland, two signals intelligence regiments of unidentified US units have been stationed on the signals espionage object "Devil's Mountain" in West Berlin'. Then there are copies of my reports from Poland for *Der Spiegel*. Altogether, it seems to have been these articles and my links with 'anti-socialist forces' in Poland which finally led to the concerted investigation of me.

By then, I was again based in West Berlin. On 7 October 1980, as the Engels Guards marched off at the end of that military parade, with carnations in their rifle-barrels, I drove back through Checkpoint Charlie, taking my last notes and possessions from the small room in Prenzlauer Berg to the large flat in Wilmersdorf. I was based in the Uhlandstrasse for another year and I wrote there my book about East Germany, for a West German publisher and audience. Extracts from the book were then serialized in *Der Spiegel*, to coincide with its publication in the autumn of 1981. Throughout that year, however, my great obsession was really Poland, as the Solidarity revolution rolled from one crisis to the next.

The Stasi, too, were obsessed by Solidarity. While I was with

the strikers in the Gdańsk shipyard, Comrade Colonel-General
Markus Wolf was in Warsaw talking anxiously to his colleagues
in the Polish services. They assured him the Polish Party would
never recognize an independent trade union. Wolf flew back to
East Berlin and rang the Foreign Minister to give him this
reassuring inside information. The Minister said: 'have you
listened to the news?' In early October, Erich Mielke told his
senior officers in the Ministry for State Security that what was
happening in Poland was a matter of life-or-death for the East
German state. At ground level, my informers' files – from
'Schuldt' to Frau R. – all contain specific enquiries about popular
reactions to Solidarity. The whole vast apparatus of the Ministry
was mobilized to find out whether the East Germans might
catch the 'Polish disease'.

Poland itself now became an 'operational area' for the East
German Security Service, a status previously reserved for countries outside the Soviet bloc. They had 'operational groups'
in all the major Polish cities and a special 'working group' in
Berlin. It was this group which was to arrange for informers to
be attached to me on my trips to Poland. There is no evidence
here that this actually happened, but I have already discovered
that there is material in my informers' files which is not in my
own. If the Poles one day decide to open their secret police
files, as the Germans have, I may yet find something there.

What this file does contain is photocopies of papers taken
secretly from my luggage at the East German airport of Berlin-
Schönefeld, while I was boarding a flight for Warsaw. These
include samizdat journals, biographical notes on leading figures
in Polish politics, maps, visiting cards, even the covers of books
I had with me – and then handwritten pages from my own
notebook.

On one of these pages I have noted down, from memory,
different formulations of the dissident's first commandment,

which I call the principle of As If. I recall a poem by a contemporary Polish poet, Ryszard Krynicki, dedicated to one of the bravest and most charismatic of Polish dissidents, Adam Michnik:

> And, really, we did not know that living here and now
> You must pretend
> That you live elsewhere and in other times.

To this I add comments by the great Russian dissident Andrei Sakharov and by a German friend, Gabriel Berger, who had been imprisoned in East Germany for political reasons: 'Sakharov: Behave as if you lived in a free country! Berger: as if the Stasi did not exist . . .' Found again, in a Stasi file.

Now I take down the original notebook from my shelf in Oxford and read on. At dawn on a snow-filled January morning I board the special bus which scuttles through the Wall to Schönefeld airport. 'Black ice on the frontier.' Then: 'Customs officer at airport. My papers gone through page by page. An envelope containing DM2,000-. His question, with a probing glance: "Is it *yours*?"' Meanwhile, as I see now, they were secretly copying those papers. Next entry: 'Middle-aged man on the Interflug jet. Woolly waistcoat and the kind of face that goes with carpet slippers.'

Another close search at Warsaw airport. Avoiding the pirate taxi-drivers at the arrivals gate, who will charge you the earth in Deutschmarks or dollars, I take an ordinary, battered Lada taxi through grey, snow-covered streets to my usual haunt, the Hotel Europejski: once the smartest hotel in town but now quite seedy. (How pleasing to find that Graham Greene, the high priest of seediness, also stayed here.) A few telephone calls from my hotel room, with strange background noises on the line. Then the film speeds up.

Frantic bustle at the Solidarity offices in Szpitalna street, ancient duplicating machines pounding away in the corner, a babble of excited conversation louder than any drinks party, workers jostling professors to get at the latest barely legible communiqué laid out on a makeshift trestle table. Round the corner, at the café, Janek, Joanna, Andrzej, chain-smoking, drinking endless glasses of tea, joking and talking all at once. '*Cześć!*', '*Hej!*' and off to the tram-driver's depot, where a public transport strike is threatened. The transport workers' leader is twenty-eight-year old Wojciech Kamiński, moustachioed, leather-jacketed, bright-eyed. His father fought against Hitler with the Polish army in the West then, returning to Poland, was imprisoned by the communists. The son is now spoiling for his fight.

Race down to the remote south-eastern corner of the country, where the farmers are demanding their own Solidarity. Wood-built villages, picturesque under thick snow, broad peasant faces, women making baskets by hand – which century are we in? Dash back to Warsaw for another crisis meeting of Solidarity's national leadership, rough-faced miners and steelworkers amid the polished wood and genteel secretaries of the Club of the Catholic Intelligentsia. Excitement, laughter, beautiful women and a great cause. What more could I want? And, everywhere, the wonderful logo of this peaceful revolution: 'Solidarność' in bright-red, jumbly letters, positively bouncing across the page, with the sturdy letter n bearing aloft the national flag, red on white.

Poland was what journalists call a 'breaking story'. To follow such a story is like being lashed to the saddlestraps of a racehorse at full gallop: very exciting, but you don't get the best view of the race. Yet I tried also to achieve a view from the grandstand, even an aerial view, and to understand the story as part of history. The history of the present.

For me, Poland was also a cause. 'Poland is my Spain', I wrote in my diary on Christmas Eve 1980. In my reports and commentaries, I tried always to be strictly accurate, fair to all sides and critical of all sides. Impartial I was not. I wanted Solidarity to win. I wanted Poland to be free.

Many of those I spent time with belonged to the Polish generation of 1968. Several would become, and remain, good friends. Helena Łuczywo, the diminutive, tireless editor of samizdat and Solidarity papers, chain-smoking, chain-talking, was a constant guide and helper. Wojciech Karpiński, literary critic, aesthete, connoisseur of Nabokov and Gombrowicz, became my informal tutor in Polish cultural history. Then there was Adam Michnik, with his extraordinary energy, his verbal brilliance and bewitching display of bad teeth, Marcin Król, the most eloquent advocate of liberal conservatism among that generation, and the poet Ryszard Krynicki, weighing every word as if the moral condition of the world might hang upon it.

There were things, important things, that they had in common with the '68ers in Germany: the casual way of dressing, the programmatic informality (straight to *ty*, rather than the formal *pan*), the attitude to sex and to personal relations more generally. But there were other things, still more important things, that were utterly different. The Polish '68ers, like the German ones, were rebelling against the ways of older generations, but here the sins of the fathers were not Nazism or collaboration with Nazism, or simply the failure to offer outright resistance to Nazism, but communism or collaboration with communism, or just the failure to resist it. Moreover, the German '68ers had never themselves lived under Nazism. The Polish '68ers had lived and still lived under communism.

Poland, in 1968, had seen a horrible campaign by the Party against those of Jewish origin, both within its own ranks and among the students – especially those who were themselves the children of Jewish communists. Now these children of the Polish counterparts of Red Lizzy and Frau R. played a part in the anti-communist opposition out of all proportion to their numbers: one more chapter in the extraordinary Jewish contribution to the history of Central Europe.

Those who had gone on to join the opposition, Jewish and non-Jewish alike, had tales to tell of secret police harassment, discrimination and imprisonment beside which the German '68ers' stories of *Berufsverbot* and 'structural violence' seemed to me, for the most part, trivial and hysterical. I loved these Polish tales of opposition. I hugely admired the older intellectual leaders of Solidarity, men like Bronisław Geremek, the historian who now turned his hand to making history, and Father Józef Tischner, with his unending supply of earthy jokes from the villagers of his native mountains. What impressed me most of all, however, was not any of these intellectuals but the steelworkers and peasant farmers and office clerks and housewives who now found their own voice and used it to speak simple but deeply moving words. It was a pentecostal moment: they spoke with tongues.

The revolutions of 1989 would be like that all over Central Europe but Poland in 1980–81 was where I saw it first. It was not a poet but a worker in Poznań, a small man with a pale face and dirty black jacket, who told me 'this is a revolution of the soul'. There was also, of course, real hardship, roaring inflation, a good deal of chaos and the fear of Soviet invasion. But this fear was often more acute outside the country than it was in Poland itself. Zbigniew Herbert, the great poet of Polish resistance, returned to Warsaw early in 1981 joking that he couldn't stand the tension abroad. I have since encountered this strange optical shift in travelling to other crisis spots – Nicaragua, El Salvador, even Bosnia. From outside, you imagine that everyone must be living every minute on the edge. Come inside, and there are normally dressed people going about their usual business, shopping, flirting, gossiping, in tranquil high streets.

This particular winter journey ended with three burly secret policemen knocking on the door of my hotel room, driving me to the police station in their battered Polonez, and giving me twenty-four hours to leave the country. I then flew to Hamburg for a meeting with the publisher and senior editors of *Der Spiegel*, and a conversation I shall never forget. According to my notebook, it went something like this: Editor, to me: 'Will the Russians invade next week?' I explain that Warsaw is the worst place from which to make that judgement. Publisher, to Editor: 'Do we have tanks?' After a moment, I realize he means photographs of tanks for a cover story. Editor: 'Actually the Russian tank didn't sell so well.' (An earlier cover had shown a Russian tank crushing a white Polish eagle.) Publisher, sprawled back in his chair, musing half to himself: 'Blood must flow properly, so we have a good cover story.' It was not my idea of a joke.

There was a special sharpness to the contrast between Germany and Poland. Generally speaking, in Poland the experience and hope of freedom outweighed the fear of war; in Germany it was the other way round. There were many reasons for this – different histories, different approaches to Russia – but one particular German fear was that if the Warsaw Pact did invade Poland, the East German army would have to be involved, as it had been in the 1968 invasion of Czechoslovakia. German soldiers would again cross the Polish frontier, forty-one years after Hitler's Wehrmacht. On the day I left East Berlin, my diary records: 'It seems to me now odds-on that the Russians will march into Poland. (And the Germans? Dr D. today says *Ja*.)' Dr D. was, of course, Dr Demps, who had just given me a farewell lunch and that handsome volume of Zille drawings.

It is so difficult to transport yourself back into the fears of that time. Because it did not actually happen, we somehow feel that it could never have happened. Yet today, as I write this, I have before me the official record of what the East German leader, Erich Honecker, told the Polish politburo member Stefan Olszowksi on 20 November 1980: 'We do not favour bloodshed. That is the last resort. But even this last resort must be applied when the Workers' and Peasants' Power must be defended. That was our experience in 1953 and it was also the case during the 1956 events in Hungary and in 1968 in Czechoslovakia.' I also have before me a graphic diagram, from the archives of the East German defence ministry, showing the army's contingency plan for crossing the Polish frontier. How close the Soviet Union actually came to invading Poland, and what German participation was seriously considered, will always remain a matter for historical speculation, but this fear was certainly not drawn from thin air.

There was also, in the West, an even larger fear which seems even more incredible today. This was the fear that in the heightened tension of the so-called 'Second Cold War' – Reagan versus Brezhnev, American cruise missiles against Soviet SS20s – the Polish revolution might light the fuse for a nuclear war which would destroy all life on earth. This was the time of the huge peace demos in Bonn, London and Amsterdam. People put stickers on their cars saying 'It's five minutes to midnight'.

I certainly had more sympathy with the movement for freedom in Eastern Europe than with the peace movement in Western Europe. In fact, I conducted a polemical exchange with the historian E. P. Thompson, that great old testament prophet of the British peace movement, on the relationship between the two. As I recall it now, I thought the danger of nuclear war was greatly, even hysterically exaggerated. But again, memory has played tricks. I am startled to find that on the last page of my diary for 1980 I myself wrote: 'There will be a nuclear war in the next decade.' And then in capital letters, as if the lower case formulation was still inadequate: 'WE WILL SEE A NUCLEAR WAR IN THIS DECADE.'

Against this backdrop of revolution and looming apocalypse, my own private life was transformed. I fell in love. Danuta had lived in the dissident intellectual milieu of beautiful Kraków, before coming to West Berlin. She was full of poetry and wonder, very pretty, very alive, infectious in her enthusiasms and in her sadness. Between those hectic trips to Poland, there were summer bicycle rides, sunlit afternoons in the beautiful woods along the Wannsee, evenings at the Greek restaurant up the road. But then, returning to the Uhlandstrasse flat, a telephone call or radio bulletin brought more news of crisis in the East.

Dashing to deliver another article to the main post office in the Winterfeldtstrasse, for telex transmission to London, I listen on the car cassette-player to the voice of Dietrich Fischer-Dieskau, vaulting through Schubert songs:

> Lachen und Weinen zu jeglicher Stunde
> Ruht bei der Liebe auf so mancherlei Grunde.

Laughing one moment, crying the next, that's how it is in love. In love, and in revolution. In my diary, the record of our own moments of rapture and crisis alternates with entries like 'high anxiety about Poland'. Our own fate and Poland's seemed completely intertwined.

Today, our sons like us to tell them stories, preferably funny ones, about life under communism and particularly about the secret police. 'Go on, Mama, tell us another story about the stupid police!' For them, these are like tales from Narnia. As for the painted fragment of the Berlin Wall which now props up some books on the landing cupboard, that might as well come from Pompeii.

Even I need a large effort of memory – or is it imagination? – to recover the experience. For the first time, I personally discovered what it is like to be prevented by a government from doing something that you really want to do. Prevented by a parent, a headmaster, by some private authority, that I had known; but prevented by the government, no. I had read about it, of course, then seen it at first hand in Eastern Europe; but now it was actually happening to me. To me, and to someone I loved.

Frontiers, visas, permits, became the stuff of everyday life, as they had never been before. Our very dreams were dogged by frontier guards. According to my diary, one night in March 1981, I dream that we are on a train crossing Poland, discussing how to get out. Forge the date stamps on our visas? Then a guard is charging along beside the train on a horse-drawn wooden cart, such as you still see in the Polish countryside, whooping 'Ustrzyki Alarm!' The same night, Danuta dreams that we are walking with a group of friends through a wood, to a frontier. We are caught by East German frontier guards. They order the group to divide: those *for* the German Democratic Republic to the left, those *against* to the right. Then they start shooting both sides. She escapes, taking, as she crosses the line, an aubergine canapé from a silver tray held by a black man in East German uniform.

That last surreal detail was probably influenced by Peter Zadek's exuberantly staged *Fallada-Revue*, which we had seen at the theatre a few days before. It was hardly less surreal for me to find myself, within a few hours, flying back to England for the *Spectator*'s annual drinks party. Or, on another brief return, dropping in to the launch of the Social Democratic Party, at the Connaught Rooms in central London. 'A rather lacklustre affair', my diary notes. And I record David Owen's plangent declaration: 'Our country is in *real trouble*.'

General Jaruzelski's imposition of martial law in Poland, on 13 December 1981, struck us both in England, staying with James in his new house in Bartlemas Road, Oxford. On the first evening of martial law, Danuta was trembling uncontrollably. Her country was in real trouble. I raged with professional frustration and sheer guilt at not being there while our friends were thrown into camps. I tried to get back in with an aid convoy but, just as I feared, the Embassy refused me a visa. 'In Poland [he] is already on the black list', a note on my file now confirms.

It was not a merry Christmas. This reversion to dictatorship, an iron gate slamming shut across the bridge to Poland, further sharpened the finality of the decision Danuta had taken to make her life with me. And the huge, the incalculable, personal cost of starting again in another country. One night she dreamed that she returned to her old home in Kraków. There was a tree in front of the house. She cut it down.

I, by contrast, was back in my own country, in the same old city. But if the city was the same, the 'I' was not. Until this moment of commitment I had still essentially lived, I suppose, with a peculiarly English – and altogether peculiar – ideal of self, an ideal of emotional invulnerability, self-control and self-sufficiency: 'somewhat reserved' as Litzi said of Kim. I was the secret soldier, travelling fastest because travelling alone. In another notebook from that time I find: 'reading Conrad's *Victory* . . . Heyst: "I only know that he who forms a tie is lost. The germ of corruption has entered his soul".' My own code, until recently. But now I thought differently. 'He who forms a tie may not be quite lost', I wrote. 'The germ of salvation has entered his soul . . .'

X

FOR ALL THE IMPRESSIVE leads laid out in their spring 1981 'plan of action' – reactivate the informers, check his mail, coordinate with the HVA, ask the KGB about renewed British interest in Kim Philby – in the autumn of that year the officers of department II/9 were still none the wiser as to what I had really been up to. However, just before Christmas they finally registered a breakthrough.

On 24 December 1981, Lieutenant-Colonel Kaulfuss reports to the head of counter-intelligence, Lieutenant-General Kratsch. 'As can be seen from the enclosed,' he writes, 'Garton Ash used his official stay in the GDR for illegal information-gathering.'

What lurks behind those innocuous words 'the enclosed'? A secret informer's report? A phone-tap? A letter snatched by dead of night from my Uhlandstrasse letter-box? A KGB tip-off? Eagerly I turn the page . . .

... AND FIND: photocopies of the extracts from my book about East Germany published that November in *Der Spiegel*. So the East German secret police only discovered what I had really been up to in their country by reading my own published account, at the same time as several million ordinary readers of West Germany's leading news magazine.

Looking through the extracts, printed under the provocative title 'Among the Red Prussians', I can see why the Stasi were annoyed. I describe at length the militarization of East German society, the size of the repressive apparatus and the number of informers. I quote from an article in which the Minister for State Security observed that the results achieved by his Ministry 'would be unthinkable without the energetic help and support of the citizens of our country'. 'For once,' I comment, 'what the Minister says is true.' I illustrate this energetic citizens' support with the case of the actor playing Dr Faust in Schwerin, who, after pouring us large Martinis and himself a small beer, tried to wheedle out of Andrea's ex-husband whether he had ever thought of escaping to the West and to find out from me whether I was a Western journalist. 'In the GDR,' I write, 'Mephistopheles may still work for the devil, but Dr Faust now works for the Stasi.'

Above all, I make an extensive and unfavourable comparison between Polish resistance and German conformity. Perhaps one day the East Germans, too, might take the revolutionary step from the solidarity of private disillusionment to Poland's public

Solidarity, 'but today, at the beginning of the 1980s, this seems no more likely than the demolition of the Wall'.

Now, when it was too late, the East German authorities sprang into action. The press department of the Foreign Ministry judged that while I 'wished to give the impression of an objective comparison of the different social developments in the GDR and the P[eople's] R[epublic of] P[oland]', in fact I was urging the 'spread of counter-revolutionary developments to the GDR'. Because of the role I was clearly playing 'in the ideological war of imperialist media against the GDR', I should be placed on the list of those forbidden to re-enter the country. They also summoned a British diplomat to the Foreign Ministry for an official protest.

The record of a meeting on 4 January 1982 with the First Secretary at the British Embassy is appended; copy to the Deputy Foreign Minister. According to this note, penned by Herr Grundmann of the British desk, Mr Astley was told that my published works 'not only contain maliciously invented lies and vilifications of the GDR but also deliberately incite to action against peace, detente, the peaceful cooperation of peoples and international understanding. This was a violation of the [Helsinki] Final Act and constituted direct interference in the internal affairs of the GDR ... The expectation was emphatically expressed that such activities, which are directed against the development of relations between the GDR and G[reat] B[ritain], would not happen again.'

In response, 'Astley mentioned the so-called personal freedom of the British journalist, whereby the Embassy had no possibility of influencing what he writes.' But Comrade Albrecht hit back. I was not just a journalist but had been there under the Cultural Agreement. Astley replied that we did not like everything the GDR published about us. Comrade Albrecht said the comparison was 'unserious'. According to this note, Astley then regretted the incident and, as a good diplomat, asked that my conduct 'should not be identified with activities of the British Government and not be judged an impediment to relations'.

The file then moves rapidly to the formal 'closing report', dated 27 April 1982. This now revises their ideological judgement. I am not 'bourgeois-liberal', as they originally thought, but 'conservative and reactionary'.

It then summarizes all the main strands of enquiry in the file: my personal details and historical research, my contacts with the British Embassy, Werner, 'Michaela' and Litzi Philby 'generally known as "Red Lizzy"'. 'It must be assumed that the real number of his contacts was much larger than that of the known contact partners.' Then Poland and my links with 'the leaders of the counter-revolution'; the airport search and its findings; my subsequent articles in *Der Spiegel* and 'the British newspapers or journals "Times", "Sunday Telegraph" and "Spectator"'. Finally, the publication of a book in which I 'malign in particularly abhorrent fashion the economic and social development in the GDR and attack the Party and State leadership as well as the foreign and security policy of our republic'. In so doing, I use 'both militant and refined anti-communist arguments'. Extracts from this book have been broadcast by the West Berlin radio station RIAS (widely listened to in East Germany), who also interviewed me on the telephone. This telephone interview suggests 'that in all probability he is again living in Oxford'.

Summing up, Lieutenant Wendt concludes that I have used the pretext of my scholarly work on Nazi Berlin to gather material to defame the GDR and, in writing about Poland, have openly declared myself 'on the side of counter-revolution'. Since I am now again based in Britain, 'the possibilities of further operational treatment are substantially limited. On account of Garton Ash's repeated attempts to intervene in the internal affairs of the GDR and the P[eople's] R[epublic of] Poland, the OPK "Romeo" is closed with the introduction of an entry ban by Main Department VI.'

For reasons that are not clear, the barrier did not actually come down for another seven months. In Werner's file, one Lieutenant Günther reports from the East German side of Checkpoint Charlie that on 25 August 1982, I appeared at 9 a.m. and applied for a day visitor's visa. He, the undersigned, knew me from the past, when I had written 'a negative article in the Western press' on the checkpoint. 'During the passport and customs controls he [TGA] was calm and reserved, and speaks only the necessary minimum with the controllers. In this, he always tries English first, although he speaks German. The citizen was cleanly and decently dressed and his appearance is neat.' He observed me getting in to a car, noted the registration number, and established that it belonged to Krätschell, Werner.

On my own file, a short memorandum from Lieutenant Wendt notes that 'on 6 December 1982 Main Department VI implemented an entry ban for "Romeo" until 31.12.89'. But how much would have changed by 31 December 1989!

I would be banned, the memo records, from entering the GDR, from transit journeys not covered by the transit agreements with the Western powers 'and, on the instructions of the Comrade Minister, [from] the specific transit between the FRG [West Germany] and Westberlin'.

Sure enough, in 1983 I was turned back from the underground frontier crossing at the Friedrichstrasse station. When I asked the officer why, he replied 'giving reasons is not internationally customary'. Some time later, also at the Friedrichstrasse station, I was hauled off the main line train from

West Berlin to Poland. Again, the frontier guard gave me no reason, but he did carefully give me back the 5 Deutschmarks I had paid for the transit visa.

XI

NOW I WANT TO KNOW about the Stasi officers. For if I and
my friends were the first side of the triangle, and the informers
were the second, then the officers were the third. What was it
like to work in the ministry? How did they come to be there?
What did they think they were up to in investigating me? What
are they doing now?

This is not easy. A few former officers have been talking
to historians and journalists. The now apparently senile Erich
Mielke was interviewed in prison for *Der Spiegel*; Markus Wolf
has become a darling of the television talk-shows. Some lesser-
known figures have formed an 'Insider Committee' to explore
the history of their ministry with more understanding than out-
siders have thus far shown. They have also participated in work-
shops with former victims of the Stasi: a strange mixture of oral
history and group therapy. One group has met regularly for
several years, chaired by an East Berlin clergyman, Ulrich
Schröter. Many of the former officers are unemployed, but some
have found interesting new jobs. Pastor Schröter tells me of
one who works as a funeral orator. He is much in demand for
the last rites of former colleagues.

I soon realize that those who are most ready to talk are mainly
from the foreign intelligence service, the HVA. What they were
doing, spying abroad, was more like what 'normal' secret services do, what all states do, so they feel they have less or even
nothing to be ashamed of. Wolfgang Hartmann, for example,
a leading light of the Insider Committee, suggests lunch in the

Sternchen pub, just off the Karl-Marx-Allee, near where I took tea and macaroons with Litzi Philby. When I arrive, he tells me this was a favoured spies' rendezvous. A sprawling, beery, wordy sort of man, Hartmann was himself an agent-runner, travelling to West Germany on false papers for secret meetings with what he delicately calls his 'partners'. His best 'partner', he says, was a senior government official in Bonn. One of the '68ers, you know . . .

Wasn't he frightened on these secret missions, with the risk of a long jail-sentence accompanying every step?

The first time, certainly, but you soon got used to it. It was really so easy, as a German in Germany, and he carefully culti-vated the accent of the Mannheim area from which his parents came.

I find that he has marvellously acquired the slightly lugubrious manner of an old-fashioned West German Social Democrat. Cover or reality? Perhaps he himself no longer knows.

Sturdy Klaus Eichner was a senior figure in the department which pursued counter-intelligence in the offensive sense of trying to spy on the other side's spies, whereas the counter-intelligence work of General Kratsch's Main Department II was supposedly about defending East Germany against foreign spies within its own borders. Unlike English, German has different words for the two things – the former is *Gegenspionage*, the latter, *Spionageabwehr* – but the experts say that in practice they always overlap.

Eichner made a special study of Western intelligence services. He says the Stasi had fully penetrated the West German foreign intelligence service: 'we knew everything they knew about us.' But the British Secret Service (SIS, also known as MI6) was excellent. Theirs was 'high quality' work, concentrated on a few individual agents and always 'gentleman-like' – he uses the English word. He once had a chance to compare the notes made by an SIS officer and his East German counterpart, both working under diplomatic cover, on an encounter between them. The Englishman's report was so much better! Subtle, perceptive, interested in the real person, whereas the East German was lost in ideological clichés. No, he won't tell me how they obtained the British report.

Sitting in his small, high-rise flat, Werner Grossmann, the last head of the HVA, describes how, in late 1989 and early 1990, he and his colleagues frantically destroyed their files. When the large shredding machines were shut down, after the Ministry was stormed, they carried on with their small personal shredders – 'like that one over there', he says, and points behind the net curtains. There it squats, the little secret-eater: a sentimental reminder of happier days, like an old soldier's rifle on the wall.

Then there is his predecessor Markus 'Mischa' Wolf, the father and legendary long-time chief of this Department of Enlightenment. Tall, well-dressed, distinguished-looking, Wolf strolls around his neighbourhood like a king, nodding loftily to people who greet him in the street. As we approach the statues of Marx and Engels that still sit – but for how much longer? – in the very centre of East Berlin, I ask him what was the difference in methods between the secret services of West and East. 'I would say, none at all', he answers without hesitation. If there was a difference, it was between the methods of both sides in Europe, which by the 1980s had become relatively 'civilized', and those of the CIA in Latin America, or of Mossad and other services in the Middle East.

What good did the spies do?

They helped to keep the peace in Europe. Each side knew so much that it was impossible for one to prepare an aggressive action without the other learning about it in advance. In particular, they reduced the danger of nuclear war. And, he insists, this was a real danger. The Cold War was not, as the historian Eric

Hobsbawm argued to him only the other day, an imaginary war. He remembers sitting up through the night during the Berlin and Cuba crises, trying to collect every scrap of information 'from our sources'. He really thought we were on the verge of war.

Wolf is everything that people say of him – handsome, intelligent, cultured, interesting, witty, charming. So the great puzzle he presents is this: being all these things, how on earth could he have stuck it out for thirty-five years in that ministry, with that gang? It's the Speer puzzle again. But Markus Wolf, the Albert Speer of East Germany, still awaits his Gitta Sereny. Sereny gradually, painfully brought Speer to acknowledge the full extent of his co-responsibility for the greatest horror of the Third Reich, the Holocaust. Wolf has yet to acknowledge his full co-responsibility for the horrors of domestic repression in East Germany – lesser horrors, of course, but still, as he says himself, 'bad things'.

He claims that he nurtured an ethos in his service rather different from the rest of the Stasi, and others confirm this. But then, recalling a description of East Germany as a 'niche society', he says that the HVA was his 'niche'. A large office block in the main compound of the Ministry for State Security – some niche! The fact is, his service was closely integrated into the domestic apparatus of repression. They cooperated on innumerable cases – as even my own file shows. He was a Deputy Minister and worked closely with Mielke, year in, year out.

Those whose business was spying on their own people are much less eager to talk. A few of them, nonetheless, have taken part in Pastor Schröter's discussion group. Kurt Zeiseweis, for example, is a regular participant. He was deputy head of department XX in Berlin, responsible for watching and controlling the capital's dissidents, cultural life, churches and universities, including the Humboldt while I was there. The classic work of a political secret police. Werner now invites Herr Zeiseweis to meet us in the Pankow vicarage.

A small, silver-haired man, with tiny blue-grey eyes and rosy cheeks, Zeiseweis wears brown running shoes, grey trousers and a track-suit top which incongruously proclaims 'The Next Generation'. He was born in 1937. During his early years his father was away at the war. His mother was poor, dedicated, hard-working – and a communist. Under the new regime, he was sent to a Party boarding school. His mother, now a local Party secretary, then suggested him for a job in State Security. And that's what he did, spending thirty years in the Berlin office, mostly in department XX.

Little Herr Zeiseweis exudes an air of bureaucratic rectitude and quiet self-importance. He says that when he spoke during the so-called 'Red Week' of political instruction at the Humboldt University, the students told him he was better than the deputy foreign minister. Today he wants above all to stress that he had high standards of conduct and decency. He was a devoted family man. He had always been true to his wife, and she to him. Their children were well brought-up, on a housing estate occupied entirely by Stasi employees. The family never watched Western television, never, except just once – when the Americans landed on the moon.

There were bad things in the Ministry, yes, he admits it. For example, the Stasi's 'Dynamo Berlin' football team that Mielke was so keen on, and the corruption around it. But he would have nothing to do with that. 'I am,' he says gravely, 'an opponent of football.' Also, people in his department talked about 'getting rid of' the dissident priest Rainer Eppelmann: arranging a car accident or something similar. He would have nothing to do with that either. Another time, they discussed trying to get a girl to infect the leading dissident Robert Havemann with VD. Again, he wouldn't countenance it.

Not he. No, he was a decent man. But once – just once – he had done wrong. During a break-in to someone's flat they found a wonderful collection of what he calls 'little model cars'. (Werner tells me afterwards that everyone in East Germany used to call them 'Matchbox cars', but Zeiseweis's internal censor still prevents him using the Western word.) The other people in the search team were stealing things from around the flat. And he just couldn't resist it. Yes, he pocketed a couple of those 'little model cars'. He did. Afterwards, the story came out, and he had to confess. 'Then I was really ashamed.'

When he has left, Werner and I look at each other, shake our heads and start quietly laughing. Otherwise we would have to cry. Here, in that chair, has sat before us a perfect textbook example of the petty bureaucratic executor of evil. A good family man. Proud of his correctness, loyalty, hard work, decency – all those 'secondary virtues' which have been identified as a key to collaboration with Nazism (and which the Prussian Association now hopes to revive). He is incapable of acknowledging, to this day, the systemic wrong of which he was a loyal servant, yet filled with remorse for having stolen a couple of Matchbox cars.

What of the officers on my case, in Main Department II? This, I learn from the experts, grew dramatically in the 1970s and 1980s, from a small counter-intelligence outfit of about 200 people to one of the largest and most important parts of the Ministry, with more than 1,400 full-time staff at head-quarters alone by 1989. Its head from 1976, the General Kratsch who appears at the end of my file, became one of Mielke's right-hand men. He was highly professional and quite ruthless, both on the job and in office politics. In 1987, he gained overall responsibility for all 'counter-intelligence' in the ministry. Meanwhile, his own department was expanded to try to contain the many challenges that came from all the new détente ties with the West. They watched not just Western spies but also ordinary Western diplomats, Western journalists, Western scholars, Western artists, Western anyone who might potentially subvert the communist system.

Unfortunately, the former officers of Main Department II are especially reluctant to talk. 'The guys from counter-intelligence are very buttoned-up', Herr Hartmann explains, apologetically. The Insider Committee can help me little, so I must proceed alone. At first, I have only the surnames, ranks and departments of those who worked on me: Lieutenant Wendt, the desk officer, Major Risse, section head, Colonels Kaulfuss and Fritz, department heads, and General Kratsch, the boss. Then the ever-helpful Gauck Authority finds me their personnel cards, which at least have first names, dates of birth and old passport-size photos. Later I get their personnel files, which contain more details of their family background, recruitment, career and any disciplinary actions against them. Gradually, like a detective, I build up a mental picture of them and begin to track them down.

I FIND MYSELF starting at the top. Pastor Schröter obtains General Kratsch's address with a single phone-call. But Kratsch is said to be unwilling to talk. His address is, coincidentally, in the same pleasant but run-down village on the outskirts of Berlin where my girlfriend Andrea used to live in 1980. He has no telephone, or at least, no traceable number. So I decide to combine a call on the General with a visit to Andrea's old home, wondering if she is still there.

A long journey out on the *S-Bahn*, the old-fashioned, over-ground suburban railway. Cobbled streets, then a dusty path leads to a bungalow with a fair-sized garden, enclosed by a rusty metal fence. I ring the bell. Frau Kratsch comes waddling to the gate. I ask for Herr Kratsch and she reluctantly lets me in.

General (retd.) Kratsch stands in gardening shorts, holding a rake. A thick-set man with an enormous belly, short-cut beard straggling down a long double-chin, and wary, piglet eyes.

I explain that I'm a historian from Oxford, that his department had an OPK file on me and that I would like to discuss the background with him: the file itself, his own work, the Cold War altogether.

He hesitates for a long moment, then agrees to meet two days later.

As I leave, I ask for directions to the street in which Andrea used to live. Oh, that's quite a walk, he exclaims, let me drive you.

Now I hesitate, but he says 'Look, the Cold War is over, so I can give you a lift!' Which he does, in his small Volkswagen.

ANDREA HAS MOVED, but I find her in the attic flat of a ramshackle villa, with a garden running straight down to a pretty lake. She looks much as I remember her, blonde, smiling, but her children are now in their late teens, carefully brought up in this private world behind the Wall. In fact, she thinks it was easier to be a single mother in the East than in the West. She also feels the political transformation of 1989 came just at the right moment for her son and daughter. They had that safe, sheltered childhood – and now they have freedom.

We reminisce, cautiously but pleasantly, about our long-distant *amitié amoureuse*. 'Do you remember ... ?' I tell her about the file and then about the wild suspicion which came to my mind as I sat down for the first time at the little plastic-wood table in Frau Schulz's room in the Gauck Authority. That evening in Prenzlauer Berg, how she opened the curtains and turned on the light.

She's a little shocked. Surely I didn't suspect her of working for the Stasi? But yes, of course she remembers that night. Actually, she doesn't think she did open the curtains. But she did turn on the light.

Why?

'Because I wanted to see your face.'

TWO DAYS LATER, I travel out again on the *S-Bahn*, early in the morning, for my interview with General Kratsch. He greets me at the gate, dressed in a shiny synthetic track-suit, and we pass through a multi-coloured bead curtain into a bungalow full of little wooden ornaments and doilies. One shelf contains a good selection of cookbooks.

He wants to start his story at the beginning, which is fine by me. He was 15 when the war ended (the same age as 'Michaela') and his father was absent, a prisoner-of-war. He had only basic schooling, then became an assistant in an ironmonger's shop. But he always yearned for adventure. He remembers seeing an advertisement in a West German magazine called *The Iron-monger*, which was illegally smuggled into East Germany and passed around in the shop. It was for a job in South Africa, and he toyed excitedly with the idea of replying to it. The way he tells me this I feel that he is really saying: if only I had! Then he wanted to join the navy. But instead they – 'they', the Party-state authorities – steered him to the Ministry.

He trained in Potsdam, where he was taught about the great British secret service, its matchless skills, its long tradition, its character as part of the development of imperialism, described by Lenin as 'the highest form of capitalism'. Then he was put to work in counter-intelligence, on what they called 'the English line'. He, a 22-year old former ironmonger's assistant from Thuringia, was to foil the legendary British secret service! Later he was put on 'the American line', and then he was in charge of the West German department. Again he had this feeling of incredulity. Here was little him pitted against the veteran General Gehlen, head of eastern military intelligence for Hitler, then for the Americans, then for Adenauer.

Nonetheless, he had notable successes against Gehlen, especially with double-agents. When an enemy agent was caught, he liked to listen in to the interrogation in the next room. He wanted to know why they had done it.

And why had they?

Partly for money. Partly the thirst for adventure. And then there was what he calls 'ideology'. 'They did it for freedom, as they would say.'

What happened to them afterwards?

Oh, of course they were sent down for long sentences.

Or the death sentence?

Yes, that too, especially in the early years. But people knew the risks they were taking.

In 1976 he became head of the whole Main Department. It was a chance to work closely with the Minister, an exciting time, although he had that one great setback with Stiller – a Stasi officer who spied for and then escaped to the West. But in the 1980s he had a growing sense that things were going wrong. He used to escape from the ministry for a good lunch at the Restaurant Moskau. Occasionally, since restaurant places in East Berlin were always scarce and tables had to be shared, he would find himself sitting next to American visitors. He liked to engage them in conversation. Little did they know . . .

Sometimes, if he'd been away from his desk like that, the Minister would telephone to ask where he'd been. Once, it must have been in the mid–1980s, he told Mielke that he'd been at one of the regular lectures in which a senior Party official surveyed current political developments and gave them the Party line.

'And did he tell you,' barked Erich Mielke, 'that the GDR is bankrupt?'

'No,' replied Kratsch, 'he didn't tell us that.'

'Well, I'm telling you that now!'

So in the mid–1980s, at a time when East Germany was being treated by many Western analysts, politicians and businessmen as the most stable and prosperous state in the Soviet bloc, the head of its secret police was telling his counter-intelligence chief that the country was bankrupt. They knew better.

When he said 'bankrupt', did Mielke specifically mean the alarming figures for hard-currency debt?

Yes, but not only that. It was also political. They saw Honecker's illusions, and they saw the contradiction between opening up to the West and trying to preserve the communist system. He, Kratsch, was the man who got the angry telephone calls from Mielke when people took refuge in Western embassies or some new revelation appeared in *Der Spiegel*. And he would tell the Minister: how can you expect me to prevent it, when we've signed all these international agreements for improved relations with the West, working conditions for journalists, freedom of movement, respect for human rights? A powerful tribute, I feel, to the subversive side of détente.

In those last years he was weary of his work. He would have retired at 60 anyway, in October 1990. But on 3 October 1990 Germany was united, and his services were no longer required.

Kratsch's own story told, I ask why they had me down for a spy.

Well, it's very simple, says Kratsch. As he has told me already, from their first days at spy school they had been taught to respect and fear the legendary British secret service. But then, from about the mid–1960s, they could not find any more British spies. The officers in department II/9 were desperate. Of course they knew who the career SIS officers were at the British Embassy, kept them under observation, photographed all their meetings with dissidents and so on. But where were their agents?

So whenever an even half-way suspicious-looking Englishman came along, they immediately started investigating to see if he was a spy. They lived in hope, but were usually disappointed.

Was this because the British secret service was so clever that the Stasi never found its agents, or because it didn't have any? Rather the latter, thinks Kratsch.

I tell Kratsch that the way he talks one could almost forget that the Stasi was an organization of which ordinary people were terrified. Had he never been frightened himself?

'Fear!' he exclaims, lifting both hands in the air, his huge belly shaking with indignation. Of course not! Not at all. People weren't afraid, they were grateful for the security! 'They thanked us from above and from below.' And he'll tell me another thing: the very first people to come and congratulate them on the Ministry's annual anniversary day were the representatives of the CDU, the old Christian Democratic puppet party now incorporated into Helmut Kohl's all-German CDU. Yet now it's the Christian Democrats who are the first to blame everything on the Stasi! Actually, the Stasi was always subordinated to the ruling communist party. Mielke was scrupulous about this. Everything was checked with Honecker, all important decisions were approved by the Party leader.

I ask if there is anything about which he personally feels guilty. 'No,' he says, 'I did my job.' The familiar defence: I was only doing my job, my duty, obeying orders. No, he does not feel guilty about anything, except that he had not been more critical of the way things were going in the 1980s, of Honecker's hubris and the lack of reforms.

'But that's the same everywhere, in your country too, if one can believe what one reads in the papers. There's criticism of the royal family but you don't have the courage to act!'

GERHARD KAULFUSS, I read in the personnel file, born 23 March 1933, in the Sudetenland. His father left for the war when he was six and only returned from a Soviet prisoner-of-war camp in 1947, when young Gerhard was fourteen. Seven formative years without a father. School in the German-occupied Sudetenland during the war: Nazi school. Then the defeat and flight into the Soviet Occupied Zone. He originally wanted to be a shop assistant but came, via the Free German Youth, to the Ministry. In time, he worked his way up to be a Colonel and the head of department II/9.

Now a snapshot from family life. In 1971, a parcel is sent to his eight-year-old daughter from West Germany: two bars of chocolate, sweets, cheese, sugar, tea, a children's toothbrush, soap. Emergency rations, as if to Biafra! Alarm bells ring. A formal disciplinary investigation is launched. How did it happen? While they were on holiday in Bulgaria, his daughter had struck up a friendship with a West German girl. 'Although an attempt was made by Comrade Major Kaulfuss to prevent this contact, by changing the bathing-place, further contacts nonetheless occurred between the children, during which the daughter of Comrade Major Kaulfuss gave the West German girl their home address.' Conclusion: this contact might be exploited by Western intelligence. If another parcel arrives, it should be brought in to the department for examination, and then sent back.

The file has an old address in Karlshorst, where the Red

Army headquarters used to be. In a dusty, run-down street, I find a two-storey, semi-detached house, painted a dirty reddish brown. There is another metal fence and gate, locked with a buzzer system – and the occupant's name. Kaulfuss. I ring. One of the net-curtains in a first-floor window is pulled back. A face appears, briefly. Is it the same as the photo on the file? He opens the front-door but waits at the top of the steps, twenty feet away. Yes, it's him all right.

'Herr Kaulfuss?', I say, raising my voice.

'Yes.'

'My name is Timothy Garton Ash, I'm a contemporary historian from Oxford, and want to talk to you about the history of the MfS.' I use the official abbreviation for the Ministry, not the implicitly pejorative 'Stasi'.

Slowly he comes to the gate, but does not open it. Like Kratsch, he wears a track-suit of some synthetic material, this one in black and purple. He has a bitter, down-turned mouth, as on the photograph, and his eyes are bloodshot. Drinking?

Would he have time for a conversation?

'No.' He had been approached by the Insider Committee and declined. All sorts of people had come to see him, the West German security service, the West German foreign intelligence service, even what he rather confusedly calls the FBIA. He had turned them all down. Anyway, it's all there in the documents.

Yes, I say, but documents never tell us everything. Conversations with historical witnesses are invaluable for understanding the background and the motives of those involved. (Perfectly true, but also: keep him talking, don't let the line snap, wind the old carp in gently.) And (risk it now) I have a personal reason: when I was here as a research student, in the early 1980s, your department had a file on me, an OPK.

We debate a little more.

'*Ach*,' he says, 'come on, we'll talk for fifteen minutes.' The gate buzzes open.

He leads me to a rocking sofa in the garden. I smell alcohol, cigarette-smoke, boredom and emptiness. He is completely unrepentant. The state was threatened by Western agents, terrorists, provocateurs, subversives. As its name suggests, the State Security Service gave ordinary people security, and they look back to it with longing now, when there's so much insecurity: crime, unemployment, drugs. Yes, there was a minority who suffered for their political views. But that's normal. Exactly the same thing happened in West Germany. What was that word they had for it? I suggest: *Berufsverbot*? Yes, that's it! It was *exactly* the same!

But I thought your system was supposed to be better?

'*Na ja* . . . ', he laughs bitterly. Anyway, most people did appreciate the security, and they didn't mind giving up a little liberty in exchange.

Was he at all disillusioned near the end? No, he had a sense of quiet satisfaction. After all, this state had achieved something: in every year of the history of East Germany there was real growth in the Gross Domestic Product. In West Germany it was the other way round. There it shrunk every year. I express some mild incredulity. He explains that the *workers' share* had shrunk. But West Germany had still got richer, hadn't it? Yes, but most people can't afford what's on offer.

Had he actually been to the West?

Well, not before unification, of course. But now he had, to the North Sea coast and to West Berlin. But he was not impressed. No. One time his granddaughter had asked him for a cuckoo-clock. So he went across to the Kaufhaus des Westens, the big department store in West Berlin. He was *disgusted*. All those goods that ordinary people can't afford. *And* they didn't have the cuckoo-clock.

No, he doesn't like going to West Berlin, after working against it all his life. But one time, shortly after unification, he couldn't resist going across on a little private tour of the Western secret service headquarters that he knew only from photographs, the CIA 'objects' in Dahlem and so on. They looked very much as on the photos.

He has relaxed, so the time seems right to ask about my file. But he clams up again.

No, he's warned me, he won't talk about his work.

No, he doesn't remember Lieutenant Wendt.

No, he doesn't remember my case.

Were there so many Operational Person Controls?

Well, no, not in his department anyway. It was something . . .

Fifteen minutes have become fifty. But now his wife is calling. She needs to be rocked on the garden sofa. She has not been well, you understand.

As we walk back to the rusty gate, I ask if his department caught many spies?

Oh yes, and of course they were sent to prison for long sentences. But he doesn't want to talk about that. What he wants me to understand is that things can't go on like this: the crime, the unemployment, the inequality. People are angry.

I take my leave, but as he retreats from the gate he raises his voice: 'It can't go on like this, I tell you, and when the call comes for us to take to the streets, we'll be there.' Heroic, pathetic defiance.

Then creak, creak, goes the garden sofa.

NOW FOR COLONEL FRITZ, Kaulfuss's successor as head of department II/9 and the man who signed off my file in 1982. Unlike his predecessor, Alfred Fritz is still a busy man. At the gate of their neat, grey semi-detached house, also in Karlshorst, his wife tells me that he's out from early morning to late at night: 'You know how it is, in the insurance business.'

I leave my card and she suggests that I telephone at ten in the evening. When I phone, and start explaining once again that I'm a historian working on the Stasi files, he says, 'Didn't we have something to do with you during my time in the service?' I tell him about the file. After some dithering, he finally agrees to meet – 'if you think it'll be any use' – at half past seven in the morning.

According to his service record, the Colonel is now sixty-five. I expect another aged, paunchy, slow-moving figure, like Kaulfuss and Kratsch. But the man who greets me, with an ingratiating grin, looks a youthful fifty-something. He has blow-dried bouffant hair and wears black jeans, a shirt with a lurid pattern of pink and grey triangles and a matching kipper tie held in place by a large tie-pin. His shirtsleeves are neatly rolled half-way up the forearms. He looks every centimetre the West German insurance salesman in his new – what? Disguise? Uniform? Identity?

I thank him for making the time in a busy day. Yes, that's the trouble, he's never been so hard-pressed.

Worse than in the Ministry?

'No. You know what it's like in that job, the evening meetings with agents and so on . . .' And he looks at me expectantly.

'You know what it's like . . .' What does he mean?

Lifting my visiting card from the table and looking at it with a smile, he says: 'Well, there are all sorts of cover, aren't there? "Contemporary historian", for example. Historian or SIS, it's all the same to me. There were several here already. I have no inhibitions.'

I assure him that I really am a contemporary historian. He seems a little disappointed. Perhaps he had looked forward to comparing notes with an old sparring partner. Or perhaps he just doesn't believe me. Still, he's ready to talk.

In the beginning was the war. The war had been a formative experience for him, as for Kaulfuss and Kratsch. His elder brother was killed at the front.

And your father?

'I never knew my father. I was what they call an illegitimate child.' He keeps smiling, but I can hear the tension in his voice and feel the old pain.

In the early 1950s, he was working in the finance department of the local government in Schwerin. He was a candidate member of the Party. When he was approached by a man from the Ministry he felt it was 'an honour' to defend East Germany against the foreign spies who were infiltrating the country *en masse*.

'You must remember what it was like then. This was the time of the "wastebin kids". The CIA would pay youths from West Berlin a few pence to come over and search the dustbins outside Red Army headquarters, here in Karlshorst.' Most of them were caught.

These were exciting years. He felt he was doing an important job. And in the 1950s they still had public support. They even went and explained what they were doing in factories, and people applauded them. (Does it not occur to him, even now, that people might have applauded out of fear?)

Things changed for the worse in the 1970s. There was less idealism, more simple careerism inside the Ministry.

Would that be true of young Lieutenant Wendt?

He doesn't know. Wendt was always very reticent.

And Major Risse?

'I think Risse meant it honestly, like me.'

There was also a sense of things going wrong in the country outside. Privately, he and his colleagues identified two main problems, the Car Problem and the Travel Problem. The Car Problem was that there were simply no decent cars available. People could only get a puttering little Trabant or Wartburg, and they had to wait ten years even for that. The Travel Problem was that most people weren't allowed to travel anywhere, except to a limited number of countries in the Soviet bloc.

Did they ever discuss the Freedom Problem?

'No!' Pause for thought. 'Although the Travel Problem was somehow related to it.'

Also, they found they were being called upon to do more and more different jobs. I quote to him a remark that Colonel Eichner of the HVA had made to me: 'We had a state. Then we had the Party to try to make the state work. Then we had the State Security to try to make the Party and state work. And still it didn't work!'

'That's about it', says Fritz.

The men from his department would even have to go and stand guard at football matches. It was ridiculous. Their proper job was to look for Western spies, although now they concentrated on what they called 'espionage from legal positions': diplomats, accredited correspondents, visiting academics and so on. His department, which covered all West European countries, ran perhaps thirty Operational Person Controls a year.

Did they actually catch any spies?

Yes, a few. Westerners were usually held in custody for a month or two, then expelled; in a serious case, they might be tried and convicted, but then probably expelled too. If they were East Germans, however, they received long prison sentences.

In his time they didn't have much success with the French or British, who were their main concern. There was one diplomat they nearly got to work for them: a woman who had a love affair which they found out about by 'B measures'. ('B measures' meant bugging, as opposed to 'A measures', which meant telephone tapping.)

Of course they tried to use this information to recruit her. She was married, you know.

'You mean, you tried to blackmail her?'

'Yes, every secret service does it.' But this time it didn't work out. The guy she had an affair with was an Englishman who later went back to England. Then, sneering slightly, he asks, 'That wasn't you, was it?'

'No.' (And anyway, none of your business.) I sense from the crooked smile on his face how he misses that side of the job: the voyeurism, the intimate details, the games they then played with a woman's life. I suppose today he must content himself with the peeping into private lives done by newspapers and television. Here's a Western version of organized voyeurism, also justified, supposedly, by some higher goal. 'State security' then, 'the public interest' now.

He returns to his favourite theme: how hard they worked. He was at his desk by 7.15 in the morning, 7.30 at the latest. He had to report to General Kratsch at a quarter to eight. Then it was reading the files, discussing current cases with his colleagues: plans of action, coordination, observation reports, concluding reports, bringing on new informers, checking old ones. Lunch, for department heads and above, was in a special canteen on a slightly raised area in the centre of the ministry compound. 'Monarchs' hill', people called it. Office work continued into the late afternoon and in the evenings there were those meetings with informers, usually in 'conspiratorial flats'. A twelve-hour day, at least, and many weekends as well.

Did he meet socially with colleagues?

At Christmas or New Year they had an office party 'in an object, you know'. For example, once they had a party in Wandlitz. 'Then the table was nicely laid, there was plenty to eat and drink and there was dancing and a nice atmosphere.' Otherwise they had no time for socializing.

Now he has to work hours that are just as long, because you can't live on the pension the former officers get. This is not the full entitlement on their actual salary but 70 per cent of a state pension calculated on the average East German wage. It's so unjust, he says. It violates the basic principle of equality before the law. At which his wife, who has been cleaning around the room, exclaims angrily, 'there's no point!' and slams the door so hard that the handle falls off. (From his personnel file, I learn that his wife and three daughters all worked for the Stasi.)

Yes – he goes on – the social security, that was one of the really good things about East Germany. And now there's all this insecurity and crime and unemployment. What use is freedom if you don't have the money to enjoy it? He sees all the difficulties now among his customers. They badly want his private insurance policies, because the state no longer provides security, but often they can't afford the premiums.

From the world of state security to the world of private insurance, Alfred Fritz personifies a much larger transition. Yesterday, the officer in grey uniform, today the salesman in black jeans; but inside, it's the same old Fritz.

MAJOR RISSE HAS moved to Dresden. I obtain his address from the local Residents' Registration Office. You can find almost anyone's address, anywhere in Germany, just by asking.

He is not at home. Looking around for something to do while waiting, I see in the middle distance a temple-like building with a large inscription saying, 'German Hygiene Museum'. Inside, there are special shows on The Pill and Aids, and a permanent exhibition entitled 'Digestion', with vast illuminated plastic innards looming above you: stomach, bile duct, upper colon, lower colon, rectum, each in a different colour. I ask a white-haired lady behind the counter for directions to the 'glass cow', a transparent, life-size model, showing all the bones, internal organs, brains and nerves. She says, 'Go through Aids into the Digestion, and the cow's on your right'.

The most famous exhibit is not the glass cow but the glass person, a woman, standing with arms raised on a table which has buttons marked with the names of the different parts: liver, heart, kidneys, and so on. Press a button and the part lights up. The attendant tells me that this is a new glass person. The old one was getting rather worn, so after unification they made a brand new person. 'Doesn't she look good? But inside she's just the same.'

When I reach Klaus Risse on the telephone in the evening, he says he would like to talk. He's interested in seeing the

Ministry's work described more 'objectively'. He has a strong Saxon accent and seems chatty, as the Saxons often are.

'Could we meet now?' I ask, late though it is, 'I hoped to get back to Berlin this evening.' No, that's impossible, he's expecting his wife any minute. But we could meet for breakfast tomorrow. Eight o'clock then, in the foyer of the hotel? Agreed. As I take a room for the night, I wonder if he will come after all. Won't his wife try to dissuade him?

Meanwhile, I study my photocopied pages from his personnel card and file. Born near Dresden in 1938, his father killed at the front in 1944: the missing father again. An internal Ministry questionnaire asks if he had ever travelled outside the GDR. His answer: '1954 – 1½ hrs Westberlin, with a friend, looking at the shops.' In 1975 he moves from Dresden to department II/9 in Berlin. From 1978 to 1983 he is head of section A, responsible for the British. His hobby is fishing.

On the personnel card photograph he looks pretty ugly, but the man who waits in the foyer the next morning has a pleasant, open face and clear eyes. He is neatly dressed in white shirt and tie, brown jacket and slip-on shoes. His opening line is much like that of his former colleagues: 'I wanted to work for a better world.' But soon he leaves that well-trodden path. The system went wrong, he says, because it was bound to go wrong, because of human nature. People can't be transformed, turned into something other than they are. Communism failed to allow for what he calls 'the inner Schweinehund'. It could only have worked if people had been angels. His judgement is simple but not shallow: that was communism's basic flaw.

Of course, he did not know this back in 1945, when they started to rebuild from nothing. His father had been killed on active service. One of his brothers was horribly run over by a tractor, dragging anti-tank defences through the village in the last days of the war. His mother, a farm labourer, saw her son's head crushed under the wheels. The family were bombed out, all their possessions destroyed. From April to October he went barefoot: 'We were the poorest of the poor.' But his mother kept them going; first his mother and then the state. He did well at primary school and the state gave him the maximum scholarship to go on to a boarding school. The state helped, but it was his mother who scraped and saved to buy his clothes and books, to see him through. His voice chokes with emotion at the memory.

At eighteen, he had to choose. He loved nature and wanted to study fishery at university. Fishing was already his passion. But they – 'they' – had other plans for him. They said: do something for the state which has done so much for you. So he joined the Ministry, working first in his local town, Pirna, then in Dresden, then in Berlin, but always on 'line two' – counter-intelligence.

Looking back now, he detects in himself a process of steady political disillusionment. He had a close friend on one of the collective farms who told him how it really was down there, in the real world. He was maddened by absurd stories in the press about the production targets of the Five Year Plan always being outdone. He saw the contradictions between theory and practice and the hypocrisy of rulers who – he quotes Heine – 'in private drank wine and in public preached water'. And there were things that came up in his work. He pauses, shakes his head: 'For example, there's something I've never told anyone before . . .'

At one of their training courses, when he was still in Dresden, the instructor read out a letter written by a woman to her husband, or perhaps he was just her boyfriend, he doesn't remember. It was such a wonderful letter, so wise, so deep, so full of inner warmth and love. His voice again chokes with emotion: 'I've never forgotten it.'

But why was the letter being read out to the Stasi officers?

'Oh, because the man was an informer, an IM.' The woman obviously suspected something, but the Stasi case officer had worked out a line with him and he had managed to keep her trust.

'That's how you should work', was the instructor's message. But Klaus Risse received, in his heart, a very different message.

He did his job. But the doubts kept growing – or so he sees it now, with the ordering power of hindsight. There were the long hours, too, and the absurd restrictions. You couldn't marry without the Ministry's approval. If your wife's father or even uncle had been in the SS, you would have to choose between her and the job. You couldn't buy a house without permission. You couldn't travel abroad without permission. Why, you weren't even allowed to grow a beard! I think of General Kratsch, clean shaven in the photograph on his personnel card but bearded now.

He wanted to get out, he says, 'but I didn't have the courage'. He had no other profession. He was afraid of the consequences. However, in 1989 he had already applied to come back to Dresden as what was called an 'officer on special mission', one of the growing number of such officers deployed by the Stasi in ordinary civilian jobs. Were it not for the Turn – like most people in East Germany he says 'the Turn', *die Wende*, to describe the end of the GDR – he would today be working as an 'officer on special mission' in this very hotel.

Instead, he looked after security at the State Bank in Dresden for a year, was fired when the West German Deutsche Bank took over, and now sells ventilation systems for restaurants. 'The Western firms came looking for us', he says. 'They knew we were able, hard-working people.' But it's a tough new world, where money determines everything and people 'walk over corpses'. There are many losers, here in the east. 'Some people

have already jumped out of the window in my apartment block.'
This Western system isn't the answer either. But he doesn't
know what is.

Meanwhile, his wife nearly lost her job when his name
appeared on a list of Stasi officers published in the press. Even
close friends had started doubting him after the sensational
revelations about the Stasi in the media, stories about torture-
chambers, where people were made to stand up to their necks
in water and so on. There were bad things, he admits it, but
they were in department XX, not in his department.

So everyone I talk to has someone else to blame. Those who
worked for the state say 'it was not us, it was the Party'. Those
who worked for the Party say 'it was not us, it was the Stasi'.
Come to the Stasi, and those who worked for foreign intelligence say 'it was not us, it was the others'. Talk to them, and
they say 'it was not our department, it was XX'. Talk to Herr
Zeiseweis from department XX and he says, 'but it wasn't me'.

When the communists seized power in Central Europe, they
talked of using 'salami tactics' to cut away the democratic opposition, slice by slice. Here, after communism, we have the salami
tactics of denial.

Risse helps to explain some of the details in my case. The article
from the Criminal Code at the beginning of the file was, he
says, a formality. However, if it came to a prosecution then the
Ministry lawyers were scrupulous to a fault. They insisted on
proof that would hold up in court. The ideological assessment
in the opening report – 'bourgeois liberal' – was important. It
meant that I was somewhere in-between: not 'progressive' but
also not 'reactionary'. These were the key categories.

How did they consult the KGB, as indicated in the plan of
action? Well, a memo was sent down to Karlshorst, where 'the
friends' sat. So they, too, called them 'the friends'? Yes, it was

quite usual to write on a file 'consult with the friends', or just, 'consult with the friend'. But the friends weren't actually very friendly. 'They treated us as small fry' – at best, as very junior partners, at worst, as representatives of an occupied country.

And the working group on Solidarity in Poland? Yes, he remembers that, he was even meant to go to Poland himself, which he wasn't at all happy about. But he doesn't think the group was very effective.

As for the early observation reports, before I had even moved to East Berlin: the Ministry had a whole troop at the Friedrichstrasse frontier crossing, ready to pick up and follow anyone who looked at all suspect or interesting.

The whole department, II/9, had perhaps twenty to thirty officers. His own British section, section A, had five men. Each year they ran only some five to ten Operational Person Controls (OPK) and at most two or three of the top-level Operational Cases (OV). So the ratio of watchers to watched was 1:3, perhaps even 1:2. How on earth did they fill five twelve-hour days a week following so few people? What did they *do* all day?

'A good question', says Risse – and one he finds difficult to answer. There were a lot of meetings, of course. The work on the OPK and OV files was minutely detailed, as I have seen for myself. The business of running informers, and winning new ones, was very time-consuming.

I ask him, as I have asked the others, whether they caught any agents. No, not in his time. 'Fritz, Alfred' – he refers to him like an index-card – may have told me about that one lady diplomat they nearly turned.

Didn't he have any scruples about blackmail based on details of a woman's private life picked up by hidden microphones?

Yes, he did have scruples, but 'every secret service does it' – he uses exactly the same phrase as Fritz.

Coming back to the claimed idealism of his post-war generation, I ask if it was different among his younger colleagues.
What about Lieutenant Wendt, for example?

'Ah, Wendt, Henning', he exclaims, smiling. Wendt, Henning, was hard-working, careful, spoke well, a good desk officer.
But he was not good at recruiting new agents because he was
over-cautious and 'contact shy'.

I say that I have some experience of this, since Wendt is
proving most reluctant to meet me.

'Ah yes, that's him all right! But perhaps his wife doesn't
want him to. You know, my wife didn't want me to. When she
came back last night she said, "You're crazy to talk to him. You
shouldn't go".'

Was she right? I think not. For I take away from this conversation the impression of an intelligent, fundamentally decent
man who came, all too understandably from that childhood, to
serve his country in an evil place. A man who did not have the
courage to get out but who has truly learned from his mistakes.
As I walk back to my hotel room to write up my notes, after
saying goodbye and wishing him all the best, there forms in my
mind a startling sentence: 'Klaus Risse is a good man.' Not just
a man with a carefully separated sphere of private decency, like
the concentration camp officer who murdered people during
the day then went home to listen to Bach and play with his
children. Not just a better-quality Zeiseweis. I mean a man with
a real goodness of heart and a conscience that is not switched
off at the office door.

I have seen him only once, as he is now, not as he was then,
in uniform, inspiring fear. Perhaps then his face really was as
ugly as it looks in the photograph on the personnel card. There
may well be things that he did or was involved in, horrible
things, that he has not told me, or has preferred to forget, or

has simply forgotten. Had I really been a victim of the Stasi, let alone a direct victim of his actions, I might feel very differently. But unless I find other evidence, I think it so.

HEINZ-JOACHIM WENDT: born 16 August 1952, in the village of Bad Kleinen. When he is still a baby, the family moves to the nearby Baltic port of Wismar, where both his parents work in the state fishery business. While attending the Gerhart Hauptmann elementary school he proves especially good at sport, so at thirteen he is sent to a boarding school in Rostock which specializes in bringing on young athletes. (This was part of the highly organized system of state support which contributed to East Germany winning so many Olympic medals.) However, at fifteen he has to transfer to the ordinary local day school 'because of a serious sport injury', as his handwritten curriculum vitae notes. In 1969, he becomes secretary of the Free German Youth group in his class.

In the spring of that year, he is recruited by the Stasi as a so-called 'social collaborator for security'. He writes and signs a short declaration, presumably dictated to him, in which he promises to 'support the Ministry for State Security so far as I am able' and confirms that he has been instructed 'that I may not talk to anyone about my connection with the MfS'. He is sixteen.

When he has passed the age of consent, two years later, they propose to turn him into an IM. The five-page proposal starts by reviewing his background and Stasi career to date: 'he delivered written reports on problems and people and appeared punctually for the scheduled meetings.' His attraction for the Ministry is that he meets other young people in their spare time. For the recruitment interview the candidate should be told how 'the enemy attempts to have a negative influence on youth with the aid of political-ideological diversion'. The officer should explain that the Ministry tries to prevent this but 'as we cannot do this on our own and according to the constitution of the GDR every GDR citizen is co-responsible for the defence of our state we turn to him and need his support'. If, as they assume, he agrees, he will receive the code-name 'Dieter Fischer'. Recruitment will take place on 23.2.71 at 19.00 hours in the conspiratorial flat of 'Chef'.

A handwritten pledge is on the file. It concludes: 'I may not speak with anyone about the form of cooperation [i.e., with the Ministry], not even with my closest relatives.'

His regular informer's file contains a few reports on teachers and schoolmates, but a year and a half later this file is closed because, at the age of nineteen, Heinz-Joachim Wendt commits himself to serve for at least ten years as a professional soldier in the Ministry for State Security. This was an alternative to the usual military service. Now he writes out in neat longhand a four-page pledge to 'conduct the struggle against the enemies of the German Democratic Republic and the socialist world-camp with all firmness'. He swears to 'behave according to the commandments of socialist ethics and morality' and to be always watchful for 'the criminal methods of the imperialist espionage-and agent-centres'. He agrees that neither he nor any of his close family should travel to, or have any contacts with, people from West Berlin, West Germany or other capitalist countries.

This is 1971. An assessment of November 1973 reads, 'he is open and honest. In the past he was easily influenced. After several discussions he turned off this weakness of character.' Just turned it off, like an electric light inside the glass person at the German Hygiene Museum.

He goes on to make a fine career. In 1974, he moves to

Berlin, to join the expanding department II/9. He's a desk officer in section A, the British section. The Ministry approves his marriage, although on certain conditions (which, however, clearly belong to the 'protection-worthy interests' identified by the law on the Stasi files). In 1984 he becomes section head, as successor to Risse, and in 1986 he is promoted to deputy head of the whole department. At the same time, he takes a degree at the Juridical Higher School in Potsdam, the Stasi's university. According to his diploma, his studies in 'Marxist-Leninist Philosophy', 'Scientific Communism', 'Criminal Tactics' and 'Imperialist Media Policy' are all 'good', but those in 'International Legal Relations' only 'satisfactory'.

His salary and rank rise accordingly: sergeant, sub-lieutenant, lieutenant, senior lieutenant, captain. An assessment in March 1989 is very favourable, although suggesting the need for 'a more understanding approach to the constraints and limited room for manoeuvre of the higher leadership levels'. He heads the department Party propaganda group, and his free time is spent on 'political and literary reading and visiting sporting and cultural events'. In April, he is proposed for promotion to major. This is formally confirmed by ministerial order on 7 October 1989, the fortieth anniversary of the state. A major at thirty-seven: time for celebration. But within a few weeks, the whole state has collapsed. What a fall it must have been for him.

Wendt is the most elusive of all. First, the Insider Committee tells me he is dead. Then the Gauck Authority comes up with the wrong Wendt. When they find the right file, and therefore his first name, I look in the Berlin telephone book: there are two pages of Wendts, none of them Heinz-Joachim. Directory enquiries cannot help. I drive out to the old address given on his personnel card. This is in Hohenschönhausen, an outlying district of East Berlin which was heavily populated by the Stasi.

I find a nondescript apartment block which used to be a Stasi house but is now a hostel for asylum-seekers.

On further enquiry, the Insider Committee think he may have moved back to his family in Wismar. Driving to the Baltic fishing port, pausing only to admire its red-brick gothic church and market-square, I find his parents in a new flat. As soon as I ask for him through the entry phone, his mother sounds alarmed and defensive. In the time it takes me to climb the stairs to their flat, she has telephoned her son. A red-cheeked, angry fishwife confronts me at the door with the news that Heinz-Joachim does not want to talk to me. 'He's not interested.' Through the half-open door, I glimpse a distraught old man. As I drive back to Berlin, I imagine the distress of parents whose son's life has gone wrong: a distress I have just reawakened.

I then write to his parents, apologize for the intrusion, and enclose a letter to Wendt explaining why I would like to hear his side of the story. He replies, from his parents' address, with a courteous, carefully worded letter.

'Of course I can remember you and some of your publications,' he writes, and 'I have for some time thought that you would one day address this subject'. However, he cannot help me in my work. His reasons are of a 'purely private nature', not political or professional. He thinks that even without a conversation I should be able to assess the facts in the file 'reasonably objectively'. 'The distance of time brings different ways of seeing. At least in my case, since I see various things with other eyes today than I did fifteen years ago or in the so-called *Wendezeit* [the 'time of the Turn', that is 1989–90].' He asks me to respect the seriousness of his motives and to refrain from 'further contact-attempts' – a sudden lapse into Stasi-speak. He wishes me 'much success' with the project.

Meanwhile, I have enquired at the Residents Registration

Offices in both Wismar and Berlin, and finally been given a computer print-out with an address in Berlin. Writing to him again at that address, I ask whether he could at least explain in a few sentences what he means by 'see[ing] various things with other eyes today'. I repeat what I said in my first letter, that as things stand I will have to write about his work only on the basis of the files, and 'for the historian that is always very unsatisfactory, since the files only tell us a part of the truth. For a really fair description one also needs the viewpoint of the historical actor.' I add: 'Also in the spirit of fairness, I would like to ask you directly: would the use of your name have possible professional or personal consequences for you or your family, which in the present situation I cannot assess?' (It sounds less awkward in German.)

I have in mind difficulties for him or his wife at work or for his children, if he has children, perhaps at school, or with their friends or friends' parents. In fact, I discuss with East German friends whether I should give all the Stasi officers the benefit of anonymity. On the whole, they think not. Certainly it would be absurd in the case of General Kratsch, one of the top men in the Ministry. Kaulfuss, Fritz and Risse were senior officers – all Colonels by the end – and are now either retired or near the end of their working lives. Their children are grown up. They did not request anonymity when we talked. But Wendt, now in his mid-forties, still has half a working life ahead of him. If a colleague or superior were to read the German edition of this book, he or his wife might have difficulties at work, as Risse's wife did after his name was published in the newspaper. Above all, perhaps Wendt has young children who might be teased or taunted as a result. I simply don't know. The atmosphere now prevailing in East Germany is less hysterical and better informed about the Stasi than in the early 1990s, but I must give him the chance.

Three weeks later, after I have sent him another letter to check that he received mine, he replies: 'So as not to appear impolite I hereby confirm receipt of your letters of 10 and 26 September.' But he reaffirms that 'for whatever reasons, I will not help you. I hope that you do not feel personally offended on this account. As the conversations with my former colleagues show, this probably does not happen to you often.' He hopes that I will accept his answer as final 'and will refrain from further contact-attempts'. He concludes: 'As things look at present, I cannot see the necessity for special personal, familial or professional caution [about being named]. Please proceed with the completion of your research work as you consider right and appropriate.' I reply saying that I regret but must respect his decision, and will send him a copy of the book.

I do regret it, not just because he was the officer directly on my case and presumably – if the ratio of officers to those they watched was as Risse remembers – spent many working hours in 1981–2 observing me through his then eyes. I regret it particularly because he was of a different generation from the others. Their careers were all directly shaped by the war: theirs were post-war lives. Wendt, by contrast, was my contemporary, just three years older than me. Like me, he grew up entirely in the divided Europe of the Cold War. Unlike me, he knew nothing but the country and system into which he was born. In its dry, bureaucratic way his file is quite eloquent about how he came to do what he did, but in person he could tell so much more. Perhaps after reading this book he will change his mind? Or perhaps not.

XII

THE STASI NOT ONLY banned me until the end of 1989; they
also put my personal details into the System of Unified Registration of Data on the Enemy, known by its Russian initials as
SOUD. Originally proposed by Yuri Andropov when he was
head of the KGB, this was an elaborate system, based in Moscow, for exchanging information between the secret police of
all the Soviet bloc countries. There were no fewer than fifteen
categories of Enemy, starting with secret agents, but including
people belonging to 'subversive organizations' and 'centres of
political-ideological diversion', 'provocateurs', 'banned and
undesirable persons', 'hostile diplomats', 'hostile correspondents', terrorists and smugglers.

I was placed in category 5: 'Persons who execute commissions
for subversive activity against the states of the socialist community on behalf of hostile intelligence services, centres of
political-ideological diversion, Zionist, hostile emigré, clerical
and other organizations.' My 'centre of political-ideological
diversion' was identified as the BBC.

According to a study made by the Gauck Authority, the Stasi
was the largest single contributor to the system and, within the
Stasi, Main Department II was the chief supplier of names.
Under 'terrorists' they listed 132 members of the Red Army
Faction and then another nine to whom East Germany had
itself granted asylum: the enemy as guest. They also entered
ninety-seven members of the Viking Youth, the neo-Nazi group
which attacked me in West Berlin. The Gauck Authority's

experts point out that the SOUD data is almost certainly still at the disposal of the Russian intelligence service – a mildly disconcerting thought. However, they also conclude that at the time the system was largely ineffective, especially since most of the Soviet bloc services kept all their best sources to themselves.

Being put into the System certainly did not prevent me from travelling to other countries in the bloc. Russia and Hungary, for example, I visited officially as a journalist. The Polish authorities at last lifted their ban in the spring of 1983, allowing me to follow the Pope's second pilgrimage to his native land and watch the great actor exhort his people to 'persevere in hope'. 'Though the totalitarian communist system remains in outward form,' I wrote, 'in reality it is still being dismantled from within.' Thereafter, each visa had to be wrung out of the Polish embassy, but I went back as often as I could.

To Czechoslovakia I travelled as a 'tourist'. Before flying to Prague, I carefully concealed the names and addresses of the people I was going to visit, writing them, in abbreviated form, in minuscule pencil letters on the back of a Eurocheque. I never telephoned dissident friends, just appeared on the doorstep, after checking that I was not being followed. I crept through the woods to evade the police outside Václav Havel's country farmhouse. Then I wrote as 'A Special Correspondent' or, once, as 'Mark Brandenburg'.

I also carried money, books and messages to the embattled dissidents in several countries. These came from their exiled friends and comrades in the West and from small charities in which I was active: the Jagiellonian Trust for Poland or our innocuously named Central and East European Publishing Project, which supported samizdat publishers and underground journals across Central and Eastern Europe. Again, I was not alone in this. Although it remained very much a minority activity right up until 1989, people at almost every point on the political spectrum were involved, from neo-conservatives like Roger Scruton (the moving spirit of the Jagiellonian Trust) through lifelong liberals like Ralf Dahrendorf (the chairman of our Central and East European Publishing Project) to neo-Trotskyites like Oliver Macdonald of the journal *Labour Focus on Eastern Europe*. As in a war, we were united by the common cause.

Looking back through the old notebooks on my shelf, I find entries in a deliberately illegible scrawl: 'Lordly invite for KB & EK?', 'A.M. for ZL?', 'Berlin-Berdyayev'. In translation: could I get a British Lord to send an official invitation to the Solidarity activists Konrad Bieliński and Ewa Kulik? Did Adam Michnik have a text for the Paris-based Polish literary quarterly *Zeszyty Literackie*? Would Isaiah Berlin write a preface to a Polish samizdat edition of Berdyayev? And so on. I remember sitting on a bench in a dusty park in Wrocław while an underground activist – today a leader of Poland's feminist movement – read out some messages written in tiny handwriting on a cigarette paper. Then she popped the paper into her mouth and swallowed it.

Possibly some of my own conspiratorial precautions were exaggerated, though since the people I visited would have been endangered far more than me, I am happy to have erred on the side of paranoia. I am delighted to have led the secret police by the nose. The end entirely justified the means; and if, on the way, I enjoyed the excitement of the game, well why not?

East Germany did not quite maintain the ban until the end of December 1989. After a forceful intervention by the then British Ambassador to East Berlin, they let me in for just two days to attend the official celebrations of the 35th anniversary of the GDR on 7 October 1984. I did notice, though, that the people at the International Press Centre were distinctly cool towards me. (I now learn that Stasi department II/13 had no fewer than twenty-four undercover officers among the Press Centre staff.)

'The city centre,' I reported, 'was pullulating with uniformed and plain-clothes police. I was stopped by plain-clothes police (*Stasi*) every time I returned to my hotel ... When I visited old friends [Werner and Annegret Krätschell, in fact] four men in a dark green Lada waited outside, conspicuously inconspicuous. Well, it's one way for the state to keep full employment.' I now find a Stasi instruction sheet which tells the frontier guard that from 8 October 1984 the ban is again to be enforced and the visa stamped invalid: 'If the object requests an explanation, he is to be told that he had received a visa until 8.10.84 by mistake.'

In April 1985, I got in for a day and a half, accompanying the then Foreign Secretary, Geoffrey Howe, on a tour of three East European states. Since I was of the party of journalists invited to travel on the Foreign Secretary's plane, I suppose that refusing me entry could have caused a very minor diplomatic incident. Again, the welcome was chilly. After that, they kept me out for four more years, although I re-applied from time to time. Each rejection is neatly recorded on the Stasi's index cards. On the SOUD card there is reference to a 1986 assessment of me by the HVA's department III, which coordinated their agents working under diplomatic cover, and was therefore presumably based on reports from their man (or woman) at the Embassy in London.

Meanwhile, Poland and Hungary started to move, with increasing speed and excitement. In June 1989 I was in Warsaw for the semi-free elections in which Solidarity triumphed and communism was, in effect, voted away. When the telephone rang at eight o'clock one morning in my room in the Hotel Europejski, the very last voice I expected to hear was that of an official in the East German foreign ministry. He rather ceremoniously informed me that there were now no obstacles to my visiting the GDR. So a few weeks later I was back in East Berlin, at the Hotel Metropol, overlooking the Friedrichstrasse station.

From there, I spent a good deal of my time organizing the publication, in several leading European newspapers, of an article I had jointly written with János Kis, the leading Hungarian dissident who now headed a fledgling Alliance of Free Democrats, and Adam Michnik, now editor-in-chief of *Gazeta Wyborcza*, the Solidarity-opposition daily newspaper which Poland's communist authorities had conceded at the first Round Table of 1989. 'In Poland and Hungary today,' we wrote, 'Europe has an unprecedented chance. It is the chance of transforming communism into liberal democracy. No one has ever done this before. No one knows whether it can be done.' And we went on to appeal to Western leaders and European public opinion to help in the process. The telephonists at the Hotel Metropol were most efficient in helping to get published all over Europe this frontal attack on everything East Germany stood for.

I had a couple of ludicrous, low-level official interviews. Clinging desperately to the ideological line on the national question given out by Kurt Hager, a man called Dr Kleitke from the GDR's Institute of International Relations refused even to speak of 'Germans', instead talking about 'GDR-people' and 'FRG-people'. However, he did daringly admit that there was something of an affinity between a GDR-person and an FRG-person: 'We somehow get on.' But, he hastily added, they also liked Britons and Dutchmen.

I talked deep into the night with a small group of dissidents in the flat of one of their leading figures, Gerd Poppe. (His own multi-volume Stasi file reveals that the Stasi tried to break up his family, instructing an agent to woo his wife and schoolteachers to turn his children against him.) They were all deeply depressed and pessimistic about the chances of East Germany following where Poland and Hungary now again led. The article I then wrote was greatly influenced by this conversation, and therefore, in the event, too pessimistic. The *Spectator*'s sub-title had me 'sighing for a chink in the Wall'. While I saw the immense possibilities of what was happening in Poland and Hungary, I, like Gerd Poppe and his friends, just could not believe that change could come so fast in East Germany and that, within a few months, people would simply be walking through the Wall.

In fact, the only person I know to have predicted this was not a dissident, or a political scientist, or a diplomat, or a journalist, but Ursula von Krosigk, the old lady with whom I stayed when I first came to live in Berlin. At breakfast one day, she told me that the previous night she had had a curious dream. In her dream, the frontier between East and West Germany was opened for just a few hours. But so many people poured across the frontier in those few hours that it could never be closed again – and Germany was reunited.

The most moving conversation on this visit was with Werner's eldest son, Joachim. The sweet little twelve-year-old in the Stasi's covert photograph of 1980 was now a tall and angry young man of twenty-one. We sat on the balcony of the vicarage, in the sweltering July heat, and he told me how he and his friends had tried independently to monitor the local elections, how the state had falsified the results, and how, when they tried to protest at the falsification, the police had dragged them by their long hair across the cobbled streets. Most people in the country, he said, were too stupid, passive and frightened to do anything. Perhaps one day change would come in East Germany, but it would take many years and by then he would be old and grey. He wanted to *live*, to travel. So far he had only once got out, for four days, to West Berlin. If ever the chance came . . .

Some weeks later, I received a letter from Joachim. The postmark was West Berlin. He had gone on holiday to Hungary and, like many others, escaped across the now loosely guarded frontier to Austria. Thence he had returned, via a reception camp, to a place within a few miles of the old vicarage in Pankow. But of course, his family could not visit him and he could not visit them – probably for many, many years to come. There was a place in Pankow where, if you stood on some old concrete blocks, you could just see across the Wall to a railway station in West Berlin. After arranging a time by telephone, he went to stand on the station platform while, in the East, his little brother and sister stood on the concrete blocks. They waved and shouted to each other, across the Wall. Afterwards, his little sister was so upset that their mother said: please, never do that again.

Then it was October, and Erich Honecker had at last been deposed under the combined pressure of Gorbachev and the demonstrations in Leipzig, now recurring with ever larger numbers every Monday evening, like contractions at a birth. The demos started each time with a service at the *Nikolaikirche*, the Church of St Nicholas. I flew to Berlin, hired a car, paid one more speeding fine on the autobahn to Leipzig, steered through the freezing fog to a parking place near the *Nikolaikirche*, persuaded the usher at the closed door to let me in to the packed church, squeezed my way into a side-aisle – and almost collided with James Fenton, his great head bowed as if in prayer. Another circle closed.

Then it was November, and I had just walked through the newly breached Wall at the Potsdamer Platz, across to West Berlin and back again, as in a fairy tale. I sat with Werner in my room in the Metropol. We looked down from the high window towards the south side of the Friedrichstrasse station, where usually almost no-one walked, because that way led only to the Wall. But now Ursula's dream had come true and crowds of people were streaming to and fro. Werner clutched his pipe and said, 'Look at that! You *can't imagine* what that means to me'.

As we watched, spellbound, we knew that nothing would ever be the same again. Communism was over. The Cold War was over. It was all over. And the one thing we did not know, Werner and I, was that he was also 'Beech-tree' and I was also 'Romeo'.

XIII

NOW IT IS OCTOBER 1995. I come into my college room in Church Walk, Oxford, and find, rolled up on the floor under the fax machine, pages from an informer's file which Werner has just faxed me from the vicarage in Pankow. Thirty pages of handwritten reports by a case officer on his regular secret meetings with IM '*Freier*', in the conspiratorial flat of 'Elisa'. The word *Freier* means both an old-fashioned 'suitor' and, more often now, the customer of a prostitute. The latter meaning is intended here. In American slang one says 'a john', but IM 'John' rather misses the Stasi's little joke. Thinking of 'kerb-crawlers', shall we say 'Crawler'?

IM 'Crawler' was a churchman, and he informed extensively on Werner, his fellow priest. The report of a meeting on 7 February 1979 concerns vague rumours that Werner had been seeing an 'unidentified female person'. Could 'Crawler' try to wheedle something out of him? Captain Exner notes:

> At the moment the IM sees no possibility of clarifying this anonymous tip in the context of a confidential talk (cosy, relaxed private meeting with alcoholic drinks). He will attempt to take any opportunity, on his own initiative, but believes that the most favourable opportunity will be the aforementioned church retreat . . . The undersigned indicated to the IM that the expenses he might thereby incur would be reimbursed.

Last week in Berlin, over a glass of wine one evening in the vicarage, Werner read out this passage to his wife Annegret and me, and we almost burst our sides laughing. How many marriages, I wonder, could so easily pass the Stasi file test?

The report continues: 'In connection with this assignment the IM once again attempted to raise a personal concern. He looked for the possibility of a journey to the FRG [West Germany], which was assured him by the undersigned.' So 'Crawler', like 'Michaela', was partly working for an exit visa, and the Stasi was again routinely using the state's Wall-tight control over its citizens' possibilities of travel as an instrument to secure collaboration.

The identification of 'Crawler' has been confirmed, in writing, by the Gauck Authority. But when Werner rang him up, he flatly denied the charge, and followed up with a letter of contorted exculpation.

I wonder if he has a fax machine?

This, in everyday life, is the process for which English has no word but German has two long ones: *Geschichtsaufarbeitung* and *Vergangenheitsbewältigung*. 'Treating', 'working through', 'coming to terms with' or even 'overcoming' the past. The second round of German past-beating, refined through the experience of the first round, after Hitler. Now again the lines of investigation, exposure, recrimination and reconciliation cross and re-cross the land. And not just this land. In the age of photocopiers, fax machines, fibre-optic cables and satellites, perfect facsimiles of the incriminating document can be flashed across the world in a few seconds and reproduced in countless copies the next day. Yesterday your secret was hidden in a single dusty cardboard file. Today it lies open on a million breakfast-tables.

Countries all over the world face this problem of 'the past'.

All the post-communist states of Europe and Asia, the former dictatorships of Latin America and South Africa. Some, like Spain after Franco or Poland under its first post-Solidarity government, try to draw a thick line under the past. Let bygones be bygones! Adam Michnik is an outspoken advocate of this approach. 'Give priority to compassion', he says, and argues that, anyway, the secret police records cannot be believed: 'For example, can we put our faith in documents prepared by Stasi informers? No one has convinced me that these documents can be trusted.'

Others have taken different paths. They have had trials: some that don't deserve the dignity of the name, like that of the Ceauşescus in Romania, more orderly show trials, like that of the former Communist leader Todor Zhivkov in Bulgaria. They have had administrative purges, like the Czechoslovak 'lustration' – with its connotation, from the Latin, of ritual purification. They have had commissions of historians, lawyers and elected politicians to look into aspects of the communist past such as the Prague Spring or the declaration of martial law in Poland. In Chile and South Africa they have had commissions for 'truth and reconciliation'.

Only the new Germany has done it all. Germany has had trials and purges and truth commissions *and* has systematically opened the secret police files to each and every individual who wants to know what was done to him or her – or what he or she did to others. This is unique. Apart from anything else, what other post-communist country would have the money to do it? The Gauck Authority's budget for 1996 was DM234 million – about £100 million. This is more than the total defence budget of Lithuania.

The Authority employs more than 3,000 full-time staff, from both east and west. Frau Schulz used to organize tours of West Berlin for the All-German Institute: taking people to view the

Wall, that kind of thing. Her successor, Frau Duncker, used to work for the East German news agency. So the Authority is itself a microcosm of uniting Germany. While waiting to see Joachim Gauck, I am embraced in a conversation between two secretaries about the recent appearance before a parliamentary tribunal of Joachim Wiegand, the senior Stasi officer who told Werner about his telephone call to me in Oxford. Secretary (east) says indignantly that to hear that horrible little pig talk you'd think the Stasi had been a branch of the Salvation Army. Secretary (west), brightly: 'yes, but I'm told it had great entertainment value'. Two worlds clash across the computer monitors. Pastor Gauck himself, like Werner, struggles to communicate the values and experience of those who have lived in a dictatorship to a society more interested in the entertainment value. This is Luther in the world of the television talk-show. I'm not sure Luther wins.

The historians in the research department are themselves a small part of this history. One or two come from the East, with hard personal experience behind them. Others used to study East Germany at institutes in the West. Several of the leading figures, however, come from the Institute of Contemporary History in Munich, famous for its studies of Nazism. Cultured, liberal men in their thirties or forties, they are scrupulous pathologists of history, trained on the corpses of the Gestapo and SS. Theirs, too, is a peculiarly German story: to spend the first half of your life professionally analysing one German dictatorship, and the second half professionally analysing the next, while all the time living in a peaceful, prosperous German democracy.

Everyone who works directly with the files has extraordinary knowledge. However sober-minded and responsible the people, the procedures and the whole atmosphere may be, there is still a voyeuristic thrill to knowing such intimate details of other people's lives. My file ladies, I notice, get a slightly higher colour when talking about 'Michaela' or 'Schuldt' or some other character in my file. Yes, they say, the work can sometimes be *very* interesting. The human interest, you know.

As I have found for myself, this knowledge is still power. Some important part of the power that a Stasi officer had is passed down to an Authority official, and thence to the individual reader, journalist or scholar, or to the employer who has requested the 'gaucking' of an employee or job applicant. They in turn must decide what use to make of it. To hire? To fire? To expose or to spare? Above all, when those two little letters 'IM' appear: the black spot. Even for the larger good purpose, even when tightly constrained by law and public scrutiny, there is something sinister about this power.

With Werner, I visit Frau Trümpelmann, a handsome, intelligent woman who prepares individual files for visitors to the reading-room in the old ministry complex on the Normannenstrasse. She describes the strange mixture of feelings among her colleagues. They have this sense of secret knowledge and therefore secret power, almost as if they were working for the Stasi. Yet many of them are also reluctant to tell friends or strangers where they work. Meanwhile, I discover that Frau Duncker does not want me to use her real name because a lot of former Stasi officers live in her neighbourhood and she fears unpleasantness, if not worse. They are still well-organized, she says.

These files change lives. One of Frau Trümpelmann's recent readers had been imprisoned for five years under the communist regime, for attempting to escape to the West. Now she found out, by reading her file, that it was the man she was living with who had denounced her to the Stasi. They still lived together. Only that morning he had wished her a good day in the archive. The woman collapsed into Frau Trümpelmann's arms.

Frau Trümpelmann, who has a Church background, takes

immense pains to help people through these shocks. She generally telephones beforehand to prepare them. She carefully explains about the nature of the files before settling them down in the reading room. She is at hand to comfort them as they read. But the strain on her is great. She has trouble with her eyes and her heart. How to work with poison every day and not yourself be poisoned?

Not all the Authority staff are as sensitive. If one were doing this another time round, one might pay more attention to training staff who work directly with the victims of repression. Third time round, Germany could get its past-beating absolutely right. But then, the point of all this is that there shouldn't be a third time.

To the end of June 1996, some 1.7 million vetting enquiries from public and private employers had been answered by the Authority. In other words, one in every ten East Germans has been 'gaucked'. In the same period, more than one million individual men and women – 1,145,005 to be precise – had applied to see their own files. Of these, nearly 420,000 had already read their files and just over 360,00 had learned with relief – or was it disappointment? – that no file on them could be found. The rest were still waiting for their applications to be processed. I can see no remotely scientific way to assess the impact of this extraordinary operation.

People like Vera Wollenberger, the woman from Werner's parish who found that her husband had been informing on her, have made horrifying discoveries. Only they can say whether it is better that they know. Some whom the Stasi had down as informers have suffered trial by media: irresponsible, sensationalist exposures, not pausing for a moment to consider motives or context or the possible unreliability of the sources. And you do have to be very careful. A friend tells the story of someone who came to him, some time in the 1980s, and said,

'Look, they've asked me to inform on you and I can't get out of it, but tell me what I can say'. Together, they worked out what he should report. But if my friend were dead, and the informer's reports were found, who would ever believe him when he gave this explanation? The extraordinary detail of the secret police files and the obsession with informers have also distracted attention from the Party leaders and functionaries, who were in charge of the whole system.

Ironically, the opening of the files, demanded by former dissidents from East Germany, has reinforced Western neo-colonial attitudes towards the East. West Germans, who never themselves had to make the agonizing choices of those who live in a dictatorship, now sit in easy judgement, dismissing East Germany as a country of Stasi spies. In reaction, many ordinary East Germans have closed ranks around figures like Manfred Stolpe, despite or even because of his being down in the files as IM 'Secretary'. My dark *doppelgänger* Lutz Bertram, the blind disc jockey who informed for the Stasi as IM 'Romeo', is now employed by the Party of Democratic Socialism, the direct successor to the ruling communist party. Incredibly, he is their 'media representative'.

Certainly this operation has not torn East German society apart in the way that some feared it would. In an agony of despair at being exposed as a Stasi collaborator, one Professor Heinz Brandt reportedly smashed to pieces his unique collection of garden gnomes, including, we are told, the only known specimen of a female gnome. Somehow a perfect image for the end of East Germany. There are cases where people have been rather unfairly dismissed from their jobs after 'gaucking' or have signed early retirement papers in panic rather than making the legal appeal to which they were entitled. However, even in the public sector many of those who came up 'gauck-positive' still retain their jobs. And not a few of those dismissed have subsequently been reinstated, or at least paid compensation, at the order of the labour courts. There have been agonizing confrontations; friendships broken; divorces; the odd brick through a window; doubtless a few blows. Worst of all, a number of suicides probably resulted, at least in part, from a negative gaucking or media exposure, known in German as 'outing'.

Against this you have to put the many, many cases where reading the files has brought people relief, enhanced understanding and a more solid footing for their present lives. When there was a public debate in Germany about closing the files again, a flood of new applications poured in to the Gauck Authority, about a thousand each day. Frau Trümpelmann, who has now handled some five hundred cases, says emphatically that in her experience most readers come away with a strong sense that this was helpful. An old man told her: 'At last I can make my will. I thought my son-in-law had been informing on me. And I said to myself "I'm damned if I'll leave my house to him!" But now I can.' 'At least now I know' is the common refrain. That is also my impression: there is catharsis, and a better foundation for going forward. But this can only be a personal impression.

Two schools of old wisdom face each other across the valley of the files. On one side, there is the old wisdom of the Jewish tradition: to remember is the secret of redemption. And that of George Santayana, so often quoted in relation to Nazism: those who forget the past are condemned to repeat it. On the other side, there is the profound insight of the historian Ernest Renan that every nation is a community both of shared memory and of shared forgetting. 'Forgetting,' writes Renan, 'and I would say even historical error, is an essential factor in the history of a nation.' And there is the everyday human experience that links 'forgive and forget' in a single phrase. Historically, the advocates of forgetting are many and impressive. They range from Cicero in 44 BC, demanding just two days after Caesar's murder that the memory of past discord be consigned to 'eternal oblivion', to Churchill in his Zurich speech two thousand years later, recalling Gladstone's appeal for 'a blessed act of oblivion' between former enemies.

There is real wisdom on both sides, and the two wisdoms cannot easily be combined. The closest I can come to it is a prescription staged through time: find out – record – reflect – but then move on. That is the least bad formula I know for truth *and* reconciliation: between peoples (Poles and Germans, English and Irish), of a people with itself (South Africans and South Africans, Salvadorans and Salvadorans), between individual men and women, and with ourselves. Of us with them, us with us, him with her – and me with myself.

It must be right that the Germans, and not just the Germans, should really understand how in the second half of the twentieth century there was again built, on German soil, a totalitarian police state, less brutal than the Third Reich, to be sure, far less damaging to its neighbours, and not genocidal, but more quietly all-pervasive in its domestic control. How this state exploited some of the very same mental habits, social disciplines and cultural appeals on which Nazism had drawn, and those same fateful 'secondary virtues' – duty, loyalty, punctuality, cleanliness, hard work. How all this could go on for so long with so many Germans being so little aware that it was going on. How the German language, that glorious but all-too-powerful instrument, once again lent itself to disguising evil as good. In short, how Germany still walked in the shadow of the Goethe Oak.

XIV

STEPHEN VIZINCZEY'S NOVEL, *In Praise of Older Women*, has an unforgettable scene where people fleeing from Hungary after the Soviet invasion in 1956 find, in the market square of a small village just across the border in Austria, a line of brand-new silver buses with yellow, hand-painted signs proclaiming their destinations: Switzerland, USA, Sweden, England, Australia. 'Where to spend the rest of one's life? A couple with a small baby, who had already boarded the bus for Belgium, got off and rushed to the vehicle marked New Zealand.'

The choices in most lives are not so stark. Yet looking back we can all see moments at which our whole lives might have followed a quite different path:

> Down the passage which we did not take
> Towards the door we never opened
> Into the rose-garden.

Each choice in your career. Each girlfriend who might have become your wife. For General Kratsch, the head of Stasi counter-intelligence, it was that advertisement in *The Ironmonger*. If only he had become an ironmonger's assistant in South Africa! For me there were, I suppose, several buses: one to becoming a diplomat, another to being a conventional academic historian, a third to being a regular foreign correspondent and, hidden round the corner, that unmarked bus for the officially non-existent service.

Instead, I chronicled as an eyewitness the gradual emancipation and final liberation of Central Europe from Soviet domination. When the Cold War ended, I set out to use more traditional methods of historical scholarship to study the events through which I had just lived, devouring piles of printed matter and spending long weary hours in the archives, reading Politburo papers which until yesterday had been top secret. Would these documents, the historian's traditional sources, lead me closer to Ranke's 'how it really was'? Meanwhile, I came across my own Stasi file and started thinking about this other path to exploring the recent past, researching history by researching myself. Here, perhaps, was a third way to approach the great question: what can we know?

For most of this time, I thought hardly at all about our own British secret world. I saw from the newspapers that our secret intelligence and security services, MI6 and MI5, seemed to be stepping gingerly out of the shadows. With the end of the Cold War, blanket official secrecy became even more difficult to justify, and these organizations had to make a new case for their continued importance – and budgets. So I read about the first public naming of the heads of both services, Acts of Parliament giving them a clear legal basis for the first time, the first ever public lecture by a Director-General of MI5 and the establishment of a parliamentary intelligence and security committee. I also saw that MI6 had moved into new headquarters. You could hardly miss that large, showy green-glass office block on the south bank of the Thames. Nothing could be less secret. But I don't think I even knew that MI5 had also moved into new headquarters on the other bank of the river: an imposing, white, neo-colonial building called Thames House, just down the road from the Houses of Parliament. I must have passed it many times without knowing what it housed.

So far was I removed from my youthful fascination with the secret service that I had almost forgotten about my own brief dalliance with it. Around the time I started work on my Stasi file, however, I had an indication that they had not quite forgotten about me. One day I received a mysterious telephone call from a man who said he worked for that same non-existent section of the Foreign Office which had made the original approach back in 1976. There was something he would like to talk to me about, if I could spare the time. We arranged to meet for tea in a London hotel.

He soon came to the point. There were, he said, from time to time students or visitors to Oxford whom they suspected of working for hostile powers. Would I consider keeping an eye on them? I told him that I would not. Although I could see the sense of what they were doing, I wished to have no such secrets from my friends, colleagues or students.

As soon as you stop to think about it – which most of us don't, most of the time – you realize that of course they must work like that. Of course there must be people, in Oxford, at other universities and in other walks of life, who have this second, part-time job, this bit of secret life. All secret services, everywhere, need their contacts and informers. And if that information led to the capture of an IRA bomb team, or of someone from the Middle East sent to assassinate Salman Rushdie, then the informer would have done a good thing and probably also a brave one.

Nonetheless, I found this approach disconcerting because it showed that after all these years they were still somehow tracking me and, at the same time, because it suggested they had not been tracking me closely enough. If they had read my work properly, they would surely have realized that I was not for this game. Or perhaps they just assumed that what people wrote was one thing but what they did, quite another. Which, of course, they often are.

At the time, this was little more than an unpleasant quarter of an hour in the middle of a busy day. Now, however, I revisit the incident in my mind, as I contemplate the need for a little further investigation of our own secret realms. What have our lot been up to? What might I have been doing had I taken that unmarked bus? Is there any truth at all in the arguments that Markus Wolf made to me as we walked around the centre of now reunited Berlin? What *is* the essential difference between the Security Service of a communist state like East Germany and the Security Service of a democracy like Britain?

Reading about spying is a great British hobby. The sheer volume of books on the subject is matched only by those on sex and gardening. Investigative journalism, memoirs, scholarly studies, spin-offs from television and radio documentaries, not to mention the endless novels and thrillers. Page 106 of my Stasi file has a note from department XX/4: ' "Romeo" arranged a meeting on 25.2.80 between "Beech-tree" and the correspondent in Warsaw Timothy Sebastian.' Friends now tell me that I must read Tim Sebastian's Stasi spy thriller, *Exit Berlin*.

The trouble with all these shelves of stuff is: how can you ever really know what is fact, what fiction, and what still lies entirely hidden? To get anywhere, I must go beyond the printed word. So after swimming around in this murky sea of print, I talk to some of those who have written well about our British secret world, to some who have now left it, more or less happily, and to politicians who, during the Cold War, had ministerial responsibility for the secret services.

My inquiry takes me down to Cornwall, for a walk along the cliffs with David Cornwell (alias John le Carré) and a memorable supper at which the Russian Ambassador pays his respects to the greatest Western spy novelist of the Cold War. I pass on into neat English country gardens, where distinguished, retired gentlemen talk to me with measured frankness. Altogether, I find in this world a curious preserve of old-fashioned gentleman Englishness: plus fours, check shirts, waistcoats, neatly rolled umbrellas, perfect manners and lawns. Light years away, aesthetically, from the kitsch-filled bungalows, beer bellies and synthetic track-suits of their Stasi opponents. Less a secret state than a secret garden. I also meet again the man who inadvertently put me off the service over lunch at 'South of the River' in 1979: cultured, witty, full of good stories and discreet charm. But then my search takes me out of these secret gardens into the gleaming white foyer of Thames House, past a large, handsome crest showing a pugnacious lion with a mermaid's tail above the proud motto *Regnum Defende*, and through some automated high-security doors faintly reminiscent of Star Trek. To achieve the latter stretches of this journey, I reluctantly agree that the conversations will be 'off the record' – that is, I will not identify those who spoke to me.

The results are frustrating. The great advantage of a dead secret service is that its secrets are no longer secret. About the Stasi we can know. The trouble with live secret services is that they are still secret. My 'South of the River' host describes his experience of spying against the Soviet Union as being like inspecting an elephant in the dark with a small pocket torch. I feel rather like that now. Those who agree to see me are glad to present their case, but openness and secrecy remain opposites and, even as we talk, they are visibly torn between the two. So all I emerge with are a few torchlit glimpses: here a glistening flank, there a horny proboscis.

Yes, East Germany was a 'hard nut to crack', say the gentlemen from MI6 – 'the friends', as I gather they are sometimes known in Whitehall. However, they did well in the rest of the Soviet bloc. They had the Poles 'almost wrapped up'. Yet they were no more prescient than anyone else in anticipating the really big political changes in the East. I probably did better as a journalist on the spot. Nonetheless, they did get at some of the other side's important official secrets, especially military ones. And this made a small but significant difference to policy. (Three former foreign secretaries cautiously agree.)

They joined the service for all the reasons you would expect: the myth, curiosity, love of adventure, travel and 'doing something for the country', as father had in the last war. The job could be very boring. Walking around the back-streets of yet another city, looking for safe meeting-places and dead-letter boxes, you sometimes wondered 'what the hell am I doing with my life?' And there were the office politics. But a lot of the work was terrific fun. That boyish word 'fun' occurs often in these conversations. One senior retired gentleman of the service recalls: 'People used to say: "I can't believe that they're paying me for doing this".' Such fun and games.

Were they more scrupulous than the other side? Well, they say, we didn't do assassination or kidnapping, and blackmail only rarely. It was so important for *morale*, says the senior retired gentleman, that our methods were *moral*. A very big word to use of this twilight world. I remember that Colonel Eichner of the Stasi described the British secret service as 'gentleman-like' – but he meant this by contrast with the CIA and the West German BND. Include the CIA's record in Latin America, and the moral distinction between methods (West) and methods (East) becomes still more blurred.

One bug is very much like another. A retired officer describes to me an authorized secret break-in into a suspect's flat in London – 'a lot of fun', he says – while a uniformed policeman stood guard down the road. His account uncannily recalls the description I have just heard from Dr Warmbier of a secret Stasi break-in to his flat in Leipzig. Retired officers of both sides want me to understand that their best agents were always the volunteers – people who did it for their own reasons, personal, political, whatever – not those who were bought or blackmailed. The common wisdom of the trade. Both describe to me, in almost identical terms, the unique quality of the personal tie between agent and case officer. 'It's a wonderful relationship,' says the senior retired gentleman from MI6. 'You can talk about anything, your job, your personal problems, your wife, and be quite sure that it will be kept secret.' I glimpse the paradox at the heart of all spying: the key to betrayal is trust. And the proudest boast of the retired Stasi officer is that he has not betrayed his agents.

So was it the different ends that justified the same means? Good when done for a free country, bad when done for a dictatorship? Right for us, wrong for them. Well, they don't necessarily think that spying abroad for another country was so very wrong, up to a point. For them, professionally, the other side was 'the opposition' and not 'the enemy'. But beyond that point, yes, it depends who it was done for.

Here is a slippery slope. How many crimes of the twentieth century, those of communism above all, have been sanctioned by saying 'the end justifies the means'. Yet the argument can not be dismissed. Take the extreme case. To try to assassinate Hitler, as Stauffenberg did in 1944, was a great and noble act. To try to assassinate Churchill would have been villainous and wrong – although the man who attempted it might have shown as much daring and courage as Stauffenberg, and might even have believed as fervently in the rightness of what he was doing. Same action, different moral value.

However, not only do the ends have to be good, the means must also be proportional to those ends. There is no simple rule about what justifies what. Each case is different, in each there is an invisible line. Did British spies cross to the wrong side of that line? Of course they did. But how far and how often? Without seeing the files, we outside can never know. But even those who were once inside, or are still inside, will also have forgotten, or re-remembered, as the kaleidoscope of memory keeps turning.

If the ethical line was crossed further and more often in the Cold War than they would today like to think, then I can guess at a few reasons. Even in my generation, people were inspired by collective and family memories of war, and by literary models of the secret soldier. Even if we didn't talk much, any more, about 'the Cold War,' many still believed that there was still a kind of war on – which, to make it more complicated, in a way there was. Things are justified in war that are not in peace. But what if you are somewhere between war and peace? Moreover, at the back of the mind, half-examined, was 'my country, right or wrong'. But what if the country was not right? Or right in general but wrong in the particular case?

Too much moral refinement can be crippling. You cannot stop for a philosophy seminar in the middle of a fight. But then you live with the consequences.

Whatever can be said of our spies abroad – or anyone else's – the harder case is that of the domestic security service. Here, ends and means are almost inseparable. Spying on your own citizens directly infringes the very freedoms it is supposed to defend. The contradiction is real and unavoidable. But if the infringement goes too far, it begins to destroy what it is meant to preserve. And who decides what is too far?

Now in case you're wondering: nothing that I have so far glimpsed of our British Security Service remotely suggests an apparatus like the Stasi. Not the numbers working for them. (MI5 has about 2,000 employees. Add 2,000 for Special Branch and then 16,000 for outside agents and informers – assuming, for the sake of argument, a ratio of 4:1, compared to the Stasi's 2:1. You can still only reach a figure of roughly one out of every four thousand adults in Britain, compared with one in fifty for East Germany.) Not the range of targets. (The Stasi had no IRA to cope with: in fact, they supported terrorists almost as much as they countered them.) Not the ways of pressurizing people into collaboration. (A major motive for the informers on my file was simply getting permission to travel abroad. Imagine that here: 'Now, Mr Evans, before we let you fly to the Costa Brava for your summer holiday, perhaps you'd just tell us a thing or two about Mr Jones . . .') Not the fear inspired. (Do we suspiciously eye the man at the next table in the pub? Is anyone in mainland Britain – apart, I hope, from terrorists and foreign spies – really afraid of MI5? When my English informer 'Smith' tried to explain to me how small and relatively harmless he thought the Stasi was, he said 'something like MI5'.)

Not the consequences for those they spy on. (In East Germany: loss of university place, like Young Brecht, loss of job, like Eberhard Haufe, reprisals against your children, as happened to Werner, and imprisonment, as happened to Dr Warmbier, with the court's sentence decided in advance – by the prosecution.) Not the political system they serve. (The Stasi was officially called 'the shield and sword of the Party', and its first task was to keep that single party in perpetual power. Even if MI5 officers have tended to lean to the Right, and some quite far to the Right, this has not prevented the democratic alternation of power between two parties, Conservative and Labour, which have in turn formed the government they serve.) And certainly not its place within the whole system. (The Stasi was not just an all-pervasive secret police; by the end it was also trying to keep the whole system working.)

A little rhetorical equation with the Stasi is so tempting: spine-chilling, sexy, a good sell. And so wrong. I'm reminded of an argument I had in the 1980s with some on the Left – 'my left-wing friends', as 'Michaela' recorded me putting it – who called their British pressure-group for political reform 'Charter 88', by analogy with the Czechoslovak human rights movement Charter 77, or their British journal *Samizdat*. This was, I felt, to misappropriate the honours of people who were risking imprisonment and even death for their beliefs. It was like pinning to your own chest a little badge saying 'hero'. Meanwhile, Václav Havel of Charter 77 was in prison again, and the Solidarity priest Father Jerzy Popiełuszko had been horribly murdered by agents of the Polish Security Service. Perhaps semantic degradation is the inevitable fate of all such terms. I now see in an English newspaper a reference to the Government whips in the House of Commons as 'that Stasi-like crew'.

However, there is an opposite fallacy: to make our own condition look better by contrasting it with something so much worse – 'Mummy, this porridge is revolting.' 'But darling, think of the children in Africa who have nothing to eat.' I note with interest that, in her lecture, Mrs Rimington of MI5 herself deploys the contrast with the Stasi. If you wish to make grey look white, put it against black. Compared with the Stasi, anything looks good. But the real comparison is with other countries in the West.

By that standard, I find more worrying things. According to the official booklet about our Security Service, published in the new, post-Cold War spirit of openness, just 3 per cent of MI5's resources were devoted to countering 'subversion' in 1995–6. But from retired and serving officers I learn that in the 1970s it was at least 30 per cent. Their working definition of 'subversion' was 'actions intended to overthrow or undermine Parliamentary democracy by political, industrial or violent means'. But how do you know what people are intending to do unless you snoop on them first?

They cast the net pretty wide. Not just over every single

member of the Communist Party of Great Britain – including, presumably, my IM 'Smith'. Also over far-left groups that came out of our British version of '68: the Socialist Workers' Party, the International Socialists, IMG, Militant Tendency. And they had files on leading members of CND and the National Council for Civil Liberties.

Ah, they say, but in most cases there were no consequences for those they snooped on. Even when MI5 produced firm evidence that an MP was a paid informer of the Czechoslovak intelligence service, the British courts acquitted him. This is true and an important truth. But not the whole truth. There was this worrisome thing called negative or 'normal' vetting. This meant that people who applied for certain jobs were checked, without their knowledge, against the files. If MI5 said they were a security risk, they would almost certainly not get the job – and they would not be told why they had not got it. Normal procedure in many Western countries for government jobs involving official secrets or, say, sensitive positions in companies handling defence contracts. But organizations like the BBC also seem routinely to have run their job applicants past MI5 for this secret vetting.

Now I recall that, back in the 1970s, a friend, the journalist Isabel Hilton, had her appointment as a reporter with BBC Scotland blocked for some time because, as the *Observer* later discovered, she had been negatively vetted. I ring Isabel up and she reminds me of the details: how the BBC actually had a full-time liaison officer called Brigadier Ronnie Stonham sitting in Room 105 at Broadcasting House, sending the cases over to MI5. The main evidence against her was, apparently, that she had been the secretary of an innocuous organization called the Scotland-China Association, which was, if anything, probably less fellow-travelling than the Society for Anglo-Chinese Understanding, to which I belonged at that time. The negative vetting hardly damaged Isabel's career; in fact, she went on to do much more interesting things instead. But the point is, she was never told that this was why she wasn't getting the job, never given a chance to refute the charges or appeal against the verdict.

But please remember, say the anonymous gentlemen, that MI5 merely gave advice: it was for the employer to decide. That is also true. The point is as much about the people in the BBC who went along with this procedure, and didn't give Isabel any right of reply, as it is about the Security Service. Why did they go along with it? Was it because this was 'just the way things are done' in secretive old post-imperial Britain, with its unwritten rules and Establishment habits of discreet cooperation? But also, perhaps, because at the back of their minds there was still the residual sense that 'there's a war on, isn't there?' We did, after all, pass almost directly from the Second World War to the Cold War. Systematic vetting was introduced in the late 1940s, at a time when even George Orwell was prepared informally to finger communist fellow-travellers to a close friend then working in a half-secret department of the Foreign Office. But the practices of secret scrutiny then became entrenched and, in the 1970s, extended to such a ludicrous extreme.

Even if MI5 officers did not in any serious sense 'conspire' against the Labour government of Harold Wilson, as the disgruntled former officer Peter Wright suggested in his book *Spycatcher*, everyone agrees that there were some very rightwing, often ex-colonial types in MI5 in the 1970s and even into the 1980s. The word 'barking' is used. What was to stop them going over the top? Ah well, say the anonymous gentlemen, there was 'the whole ethos of the service', 'our attitudes', the 'kind of people we are'. Shades of a housemaster at school. Also, they were closely supervised by the Home Office: warrants for phone-taps, mail-interceptions and break-ins had to be signed by the Home Secretary. The Home Office was no walk-over, you can be sure.

Well, perhaps not; even Peter Wright gives some testimony to the strictness of Home Office scrutiny. But is that really all it hung upon? On what one set of chaps thought was 'reasonable' and 'decent', checked by another set of chaps in the Home Office and occasionally by the home secretary or prime minister – who were, after all, party politicians. A pretty slender thread, even if drawn from best British worsted.

These habits and attitudes matter. Laws and parliamentary controls are no guarantee without them. But why couldn't we have both?

Things have changed since the world changed in 1989. At last there are laws regulating the individual services, Commissioners and Tribunals to which you can complain, and the parliamentary committee. There is a little guarded openness. According to new rules, people should always be told when they are being vetted. I have the impression of better management, more professionalism. I'm sure most of MI5's work is against serious threats like IRA bombers, other terrorists, foreign spies and now also against organized crime. There's a real danger of liberal hypocrisy here: denouncing our spooks and narks while enjoying the security they help to provide. Kipling's 'makin' mock o' uniforms that guard you while you sleep' – except these soldiers wear no uniform.

Yet made sensitive, perhaps over-sensitive, by the Stasi experience, I find things that worry me still. I start talking to a senior serving officer about these new legal and parliamentary forms of control. 'You use the word control,' he says, 'I prefer to talk of validation.' MI5 decides what are the main threats to national security; others validate their priorities. Can this be right?

These gentlemen radiate a sense of quiet power: the power that comes, that has always come, that always will come, from secret knowledge. This power must be enhanced by new technologies. As we talk, I spy – to use a possibly appropriate phrase – a very large computer screen in the corner of the office, with an array of icons even more impressive than that on the Power Mac my children use at home. Our icons have the titles of computer games: Discworld, SimCity2000, Lemmings. I wonder what's their game?

Soon, I suppose, the information will all be on computer. What will happen then to the paper files that were once – we read – cheerfully mustered by pretty young debutantes traipsing around the old MI5 Registry? Altogether, I want to know more about their files, at once the historian's and the secret policeman's treasure.

For a start, how many files do they have?

Answer: 'In the low hundreds of thousands.'

This seems to me an awful lot of files for a free country. (And that doesn't include the personal data held by Special Branch, said to cover as many as 2 million names.)

Why so many?

Well, please remember that during the Cold War they tried to keep tabs on every Communist and almost every Russian in this country. That was a lot of people. Then there are Irish and other terrorists. Oh yes, and about one in five of the files is on 'non-adversarial' persons, friendly contacts of various kinds.

Moreover, only a small proportion of these files is being actively worked on at any time. They have rigorous rules for when to open a file, and how long it can stay open. In fact, they have a traffic-light system: green for active investigation; amber means you don't actively investigate, but add to it things that come your way; red files are closed.

Yes, but the red files are not actually destroyed are they?

No.

And would they be used in vetting?

Well, yes. But the record of some political peccadillo long ago would not lead them to assess you as a security threat now.

Can outside organizations still come to them to vet their job applicants?

Yes, but only those on a government-approved list of 'consumers'.

Is the BBC still on the list?

A sudden vagueness sets in.

These are glimpses, I repeat, just glimpses, by the light of a small pocket torch. Here I know in advance that I can never really know – unless the British state collapses like East Germany, which I certainly don't wish. But there is one small discovery that I do make, just for myself. Coming to this through my Stasi file, I naturally want to know whether MI5 also have a file on me. I don't really expect to find out, but here I am, so I pop the question.

'Do you have a file on me?'

A slight pause. An intake of breath. A man suspended between openness and secrecy. Then: 'Yes, since you ask, we do. We have what's called a white card file on you.' That means: non-adversarial.

They have me down as having 'assisted SIS'.

Well, I exclaim, I didn't *assist* SIS. I nearly joined when I was young and then decided not to, that's all.

I mention the little approach to me more recently. Would that have been MI5? 'No, that would be over there', he says, and nods across the Thames, towards the green-glass headquarters of SIS (MI6) on the other bank. However, some record of that would also be on the file, together with a note on a couple of conversations I have had on the way here.

But, he says, this is the first time he's told anyone that they have a file. And already he seems worried by having done so. Has he gone too far with the new openness?

Incidentally, I'm quoting from the notes I made immediately afterwards – as I did for my conversations with 'Michaela' and General Kratsch and all the rest. In this case, however, I trust that my interlocutors have a precise record of our conversation, although no tape-recorder was visible on their spotless coffee-table.

Now, suppose I'd had an adversarial file. After all, if Isabel Hilton was negatively judged for being secretary of the Scotland-China Association, I was a member of the Society for Anglo-Chinese Understanding. Would they have told me about that?

'Well, we don't tell anybody . . .' A dry half-laugh. 'Except you just now.'

But if I were American, I could apply to read my FBI file under the Freedom of Information Act. Why not here?

Yes, well, for a start, that would double MI5's budget at a stroke. The Americans have found that it's a huge amount of work. (All that sifting, copying and blacking-out – and I think of the more than 3,000 employees of the Gauck Authority.)

But the Americans have the money. (A small undertone of resentment there.)

And then, it would be very difficult because the IRA, foreign terrorists and other enemies could get valuable clues, even from other people's files, about the way MI5 works. (I think: yes, that's probably true.)

What about much older files, for the historians?

Well, even that's difficult. Sets a precedent. Gives clues to

operational methods. Still, they are trying to help. They hope
to open some files from the First World War.

Later, after discussing some more general questions, I ask
point blank: Can I read my file?

No.

Why not?

Because it's the property of the Crown.

In most countries you cannot see the file the security service
has on you, but where else in the world would you be offered
that explanation? The Crown!

They give a couple more reasons. It could set a precedent.
It might compromise covert sources. But who on earth could
they be – covert sources, on me? Surely not colleagues or
friends? Surely. Could it be that those friendly British 'diplomats', at the Embassy in wherever, have added a few reports?
Or perhaps there is actually little or nothing on the file between,
say, 1979, when I decided not to join, and 1994, when they
approached me again?

Anyway, the other man adds helpfully, opening files on
friendly contacts is also a matter of simple politeness. Wouldn't
it be awful if someone rang up and we couldn't remember who
he was?

How frightfully English: 'We did open a file on you, old boy
– just a matter of politeness.'

On the train back to Oxford I interrogate myself. What do I
feel? First, satisfaction at an unexpectedly successful enquiry.
Why, if the man is to be believed, I may be the first person in
Britain ever to have found out, simply by asking, that he has a
file. And at the same time, anger. Anger that they are still
keeping tabs on me, however lightly. Also, some minor irri-
tation. How much neater it would be if they could have had an
adversarial file on me. Then one could say: 'See, both the Stasi

and MI5 were following me, what a fearless all-round dissident I must be!' (A lot of boasting goes on around secret files.) But life isn't like that, most of the time anyway. It's more complicated. The past is never quite past. Years later, some half-forgotten thing you did when you were young catches up. Somewhere, perhaps, there is your own child, growing up with someone else as his father. Or a file, growing too. And you never knew.

How many of us would face a little surprise if the British files were ever opened? Secret file-makers do see things in their own special light. I never in my life consciously 'assisted' MI6, yet now I'm told this is the general category under which I'm filed. And I think of the East Germans who discovered, when the files were opened, that the Stasi had filed them as friendly contacts or even as informers. Some of them only pretended they didn't know or had suppressed the memory. But some genuinely did not know; they were innocent.

For a moment, I imagine 'Michaela' turning round and saying: 'Well, you see, your own Security Service had you down as a British IM!' Rubbish, of course. What she did was to talk regularly, at length and in detail about colleagues, friends and family, to someone she knew was a secret police officer. I did nothing of the kind – and anyway, it wouldn't be the same even if I had 'assisted' MI6. Assisting the foreign intelligence service of a democracy like Britain against a dictatorship like East Germany is not the same as informing for the domestic secret police of that dictatorship. Yet if I write this up honestly, I shall throw myself open even to that absurd comparison.

Continuing this self-interrogation on the 5.20 from Paddington, I ask myself: but would you really have wanted to be down in the files as a past 'adversary'? Would you seriously wish to have had the politics that would have put you there, rather than the liberal politics you did have and still do?

'Bourgeois liberal', as the opening report on the Stasi file rightly judged. After all, you support this system, don't you? Parliamentary democracy, for all its faults. Yes, comes the immediate reply, but I support it in my own way.

We are told that many spies have something of the writer in them, and many writers certainly have something of the spy. The domestic spies in a free country live this professional paradox: they infringe our liberties in order to protect them. But we have another paradox: we support the system by questioning it. That's where I stand.

XV

DECEMBER 1996 and I am back in my room. Journey's end. The old-fashioned cardboard binder on Frau Schulz's table has become a 'Word' file in the computer before me. There is a cup of coffee at my right hand, next to the mouse. Winter sunlight slants through the blinds. I swivel round and think.

My investigation of the Stasi's investigation of me has led me back, down strange side-alleys and thorny paths, deep into many pasts: other countries', other people's and my own. For years I have been wondering at the seemingly infinite capacity of Central European memories: the capacity to forget. Again and again, we find ourselves watching with incredulity as some-one like Kurt Waldheim, the former Austrian President, just 'cannot remember' whole patches of his past, until he is gradually, painfully 'reminded' by successive documents or testimonies.

Now the galling thing is to discover how much I myself have forgotten of my own life. Even today, when I have this minute documentary record – the file, the diary, the letters – I can still only grope towards an imaginative reconstruction of that past me. For each individual self is built, like Renan's nations, through this continuous remixing of memory and forgetting. But if I can't even work out what I myself was like fifteen years ago, what chance have I of writing anyone else's history?

Who was he, this young Romeo, yomping around Berlin in his heavy Oxford shoes? Like Frau Schulz, everyone giggles at the code-name. West German journalists used to describe the

Stasi agents that Markus Wolf sent to seduce lonely secretaries in Bonn as 'Romeos'. But that's a travesty of Romeo. The real Romeo, Shakespeare's Romeo, is no Don Juan or Casanova, let alone some picayune East German version of James Bond. He's not a cynical womanizer but a young romantic: hot-headed, well-meaning, idealistic and confused.

In this sense, my code-name – which probably derived, I still insist, from my Alfa-Romeo car – was curiously apt. For romantic I was, and not just about love. Romanticism, as Laurenz Demps wryly observed, can be dangerous. The romantic can so easily hurt by trying to help, as Romeo did for his friend Mercutio, while trying to stop his fight with Tybalt. Or he may do damage for the sake of adventure, or throw himself into the service of a bad cause.

Although an East German prosecutor could certainly have argued that I was collecting information for 'foreign organizations', in the deliberately vague wording of Article 97 of the Criminal Code, I was probably never at risk of the prescribed jail sentence of 'not less than five years', let alone of the death sentence envisaged in 'especially serious cases'. By the 1980s, the usual measure against lesser enemies was what finally happened to me: expulsion. But I might have done more serious harm to the people I met. Werner, for example, was being investigated under Article 100, which covers the offence of aiding those identified in Article 97 – meaning, in this case, me. The recommended sentence was between one and ten years in prison.

As to my support for Solidarity and the anti-communist dissidents of Central Europe, well, the history of the twentieth century is strewn with the moral remains of men and women who have gone astray through romantic involvement with a political struggle in a faraway country – whether Che Guevara's guerrillas, or the Viet Cong, or either side in the Spanish civil war, or the communist struggle against fascism in Europe. Look at young Kim Philby, led on by Litzi in Vienna. Or Frau R., who ended up as a Stasi informer. Youthful idealism can come to that.

I was just so lucky. Lucky in the country of my birth. Lucky in my privileged background, my parents, my education. Lucky in true friends like James and Werner. Lucky in my Juliet. Lucky in my choice of profession. Lucky, too, in my cause. For the Central European struggle against communism was a good cause. Born a few years earlier, and I might have been backing the Khmer Rouge against the Americans. Born to a poor family in Bad Kleinen, East Germany, and I might have been Lieutenant Wendt.

In 1939, Thomas Mann wrote a great essay entitled 'Brother Hitler'. Mann discovered in the self-professed 'artist' Adolf Hitler some elements of what he himself regarded, by introspection, as the artistic temperament. In this sense, he said, he had reluctantly to recognize Hitler as his 'brother'. I can't quite bring myself to say 'Brother Romeo' of the man who informed for the Stasi as IM 'Romeo' and is now media representative for the post-communists. But I can understand each of the informers on my file, and the officers too, even Kratsch. For when they tell their stories you can see so clearly how they came to do what they did: in a different time, a different place, a different world.

What you find here, in the files, is how deeply our conduct is influenced by our circumstances. How *large* of all that human hearts endure, that part which laws or kings can cause or cure. What you find is less malice than human weakness, a vast anthology of human weakness. And when you talk to those involved, what you find is less deliberate dishonesty than our almost infinite capacity for self-deception.

If only I had met, on this search, a single clearly evil person.

But they were all just weak, shaped by circumstance, self-deceiving; human, all too human. Yet the sum of all their actions was a great evil. It's true what people often say: we, who never faced these choices, can never know how we would have acted in their position, or would act in another dictatorship. So who are we to condemn? But equally: who are we to forgive? 'Do not forgive,' writes the Polish poet Zbigniew Herbert,

> Do no forgive, for truly it is not in your power to forgive
> In the name of those who were betrayed at dawn.

These Stasi officers and informers had victims. Only their victims have the right to forgive.

The file is a gift. As I close it, I take away a new version of the principle of As If. The East European dissidents' principle of As If said: try to live in this dictatorship as if you were in a free country! As if the Stasi did not exist. My new principle of As If is the opposite: try to live in this free country as if the Stasi were always watching you! Imagine your wife, or your best friend, reading the Stasi record of what you said about them to another friend last Saturday night, or of what you did in Amsterdam last week. Can you live so you would not be embarrassed by it? Not seriously embarrassed, I mean. A little embarrassment will be unavoidable, such is the crooked timber of humanity.

What is it that makes one person a Stauffenberg, another a Speer? Twenty years on, I am little closer to an answer. A clear value system or faith? Reason and experience? Sheer physical strength or weakness? Firm roots in a family, community, nation? There is no simple rule, no single explanation. Yet as those who worked for the secret police talk to me about their lives I feel again and again that the key lies in their childhood. I think, for example, that Major Risse was saved, as a human being, by his mother's love. But what touches me most, being a father, is the part of the fathers.

This is so obvious in post-war Germany. There is the absent father: away at the war, killed on active service, or somewhere in a prisoner-of-war camp. There is the father who was a Nazi or the father who was a victim of the Nazis. The psychological legacy of Nazism and war prepares the candidates for the next round of dictatorship. Then, in those vulnerable years between childhood and maturity, the young Romeo years, they are caught.

Sometimes, quite often in fact, the Stasi comes as a substitute father. You are invited into the headmaster's office. He introduces you to an elderly man, dignified, inspiring, a war veteran. The old man appeals to your patriotism, youthful ambition and thirst for adventure. Your case officer is the father you never knew. But evil does not confine itself to one tune. Like *Erlkönig*, the elf king in Schubert's tremendous setting of Goethe's poem, evil woos in many guises and with such diverse charms: sweet music, bright flowers, golden robes and great games.

I am the father now. In just a few years' time, as the century ends, my own sons will set off on that perilous journey between childhood and maturity, each to their own personal Berlin. With luck, they will never have to confront the extreme choices that so many had to face in Europe over this rotten twentieth century: to be a Stauffenberg or to be a Speer. But they will face many lesser choices and the elf king will be waiting for them, in the shadows by the roadside.

How to arm them for their journey? Unlike those lost children whom the Stasi gathered in, they will have bags of love under their saddle, mother's to one side, father's to the other. But will that be enough? They will also have education, a knowledge of other times, countries and beliefs. My Stasi officers, narrowly brought up in an impoverished, occupied land, then stuck behind the Wall, had so little of that from which to question the world-view they were fed from above.

Of course, it is possible to have wider knowledge and still to persecute others for thinking or behaving differently from you, but it is, at least, less likely. This is the lesson of my other Berlin, the philosopher not the city. Recognizing the diversity of human cultures, seeing that people pursue goals that cannot be reconciled, we acknowledge the relativity of our own ways and beliefs. This makes for tolerance. But in the peroration of his greatest essay, Isaiah Berlin quotes another writer: 'To realise the relative validity of one's convictions and yet stand for them unflinchingly is what distinguishes a civilized man from a barbarian.'

Here is the more difficult part. From what source can we derive those standards of right and wrong strong enough to challenge, if need be, the very system we have been brought up to accept as right, and to counter the deep normative power of the given? Where to find the courage to defend these values 'unflinchingly', even to the death, if we know all along that they are only relative? And how to impart not just the values but also the courage to our children?

I place a compact disc in the computer's CD-drive, and click the 'play' button on screen. From a loudspeaker somewhere behind the text I have just typed there comes the voice of Dietrich Fischer-Dieskau, recorded in 1958, at the height of the Cold War, singing Schubert's great dark song. Can any father hear it and not be moved?

Through night and wind the father rides, his child in his arms. He holds him fast, he keeps him warm. The voice is strong and firm. Then the elf king comes out of the night, and woos the child with such beautiful lines: about those bright flowers, golden robes and great games, about his daughters who will cradle you and dance with you and sing you to sleep. And if you're not willing – the voice is suddenly harsh – he must then use force. Against the music's threatening insistence the child cries out: 'Oh father, father, he's seizing me now.' The father rides for dear life. He reaches home at last. The voice sinks almost to nothing: 'In his arms . . . the child . . . was . . . dead.'

I save the file called Romeo on my computer and close the door. I go to my sons.

Afterword (2009)

In the twelve years since this book first appeared, 'Stasi' has become a global synonym for secret police terror. 'Hitler is Germany's best export product,' a German critic once remarked, but the Stasi is chasing him fast. Stasi and Nazi are now mentioned in the same breath, and in English they are almost made to rhyme.

Ironically, this worldwide identification of Germany with another version of evil is a result of democratic Germany's own exemplary commitment to expose all the facts about its second twentieth-century dictatorship, not brushing anything under the carpet. This was probably the most swift and scrupulous documentation of any dictatorship in history. Yet, by stages, the Stasi has passed from history to something approaching myth.

For many people I meet, an important stage in that mnemonic transition was watching the film *The Lives of Others*. I've written about *The Lives of Others* elsewhere, and I won't repeat myself.* It is a brilliant, compelling and useful film, but it does quite consciously take East Germany to Hollywood. The reality, as I have tried to capture it here, was more banal. Hannah Arendt's phrase 'the banality of evil' has itself become a banality; it nonetheless contains a necessary warning. Evil usually does not come wearing leather boots and a whip.

Anyway, the result is this: say 'East Germany' to someone in any corner of the world today, and their reaction, if they have any at all, will likely as not be 'Stasi'. So widespread and automatic has this cognitive association become that I sometimes want to protest.

---

* See my essay 'The Stasi on Our Minds' in Timothy Garton Ash, *Facts are Subversive: Political Writing from a Decade Without a Name* (London: Atlantic Books, 2009).

In 1979, when many Western observers were downplaying or ignoring the Stasi, I felt impelled to insist: this is still a secret police state. Don't forget the Stasi! In 2009, I want to say: yes, but East Germany was not only the Stasi.

This book moves to and fro between Britain and Germany. To the German part of the story, I have little to add. In one respect I wish I had. I would still like to talk to Heinz-Joachim Wendt, the Stasi officer most directly involved in compiling my file, and the only one who refused to meet me. Earlier this year, anticipating the twentieth anniversary of the fall of the Berlin Wall, I made another attempt to contact him – in Stasi jargon this would be called a *Kontaktversuch* – through my old friend Werner Krätschell (a.k.a. 'Beech-Tree'). In an e-mail, Wendt politely but firmly declined, citing his 'north German stubbornness' and the fact that 'after twenty years the memories do slowly fade'. Perhaps in 2029, if my north European stubbornness finally wears down his, we shall sit opposite each other, two old men in some dreary café, and find we remember nothing at all. Or perhaps Memory, that novelist in everyone's head, will by then have consummated the transubstantiation of fact into fiction.

In his e-mail, Wendt mentioned in passing one detail which was new to me. He recalled that the minister for state security, Erich Mielke, 'took personal offence' at some passage in my original book about East Germany, which was serialized in the leading West German news magazine *Der Spiegel*, and therefore no longer 'wished to tolerate my presence' in the GDR. So when my file says, in a note signed by Lieutenant Wendt and dated 6 January 1982, that I would be banned not just from the GDR but also from the transit routes between West Germany and West Berlin 'on the instructions of the Comrade Minister', that was not, as I had imagined, a mere bureaucratic formality. It was personal. Good. I hope reading that extract in *Der Spiegel* thoroughly spoiled the Comrade Minister's breakfast. But Mielke is dead, and this is all ancient history.

As to the British part of *The File*, I wish there was no more to add – but unfortunately there is. For when the word 'Stasi' pops up in Britain today, it's usually in the context of the erosion of civil liberties and privacy in what used to be one of the most free countries in the world. At a rousing Convention on Modern Liberty in early 2009, Shami Chakrabarti, the head of the campaigning organization Liberty, contrasted British complacency with the attitude of – as a transcript on the Convention's website records her words – 'Continental people with memories of the Nazis and the Stazi'. (Sitting in the audience, I heard her say, 'Nazis and Stazis', which almost perfects the rhyme.) A diary item in the *Financial Times* reports a warning by a former head of Britain's Security Service, no less, that Britain is in danger of becoming a police state. The piece is headed 'Stasi state'. No explanation needed. Everyone will get the reference.

Everyone understands, too, unless they are very stupid or paranoid, that Britain is not actually a Stasi state. But since this book was first published in 1997, the year New Labour came to power, two sets of developments have converged to give real cause for alarm. One set is technological, the other political. Technologically, these developments include computer databases, CCTV cameras, individual e-mail and web search records, mobile phone records and tracking, computerized medical and credit card histories, a government DNA database, biometric indicators, the personal information on social networking sites such as Facebook and MySpace, pinpoint satellite photography, miniature and super-sensitive directional microphones – need I go on? Putting these together, in what is now called 'data mining' or 'reality mining', gives both the state and private companies possibilities of surveillance and intrusion into individuals' private lives – yours, mine, everyone's – that Erich Mielke could not have fantasized in his wettest dreams. Just imagine what the Stasi would have done with it. So the technological *potential* for control has grown exponentially.

Politically, especially since the terrorist attacks on New York, London and Madrid, both the covert use of these technologies and explicit restrictions on individual liberty, including detention without trial, curbs on free speech and legalized invasions of privacy, have been extended by the British government in the name of enhancing national security and the safety of individual citizens. This tendency to put security before liberty has been seen in other areas, too, such as ridiculous petty regulations – treating grown-ups like children, and children like babies – imposed on grounds of 'health and safety'. Other governments of liberal democracies have travelled some way down these roads, but few so far and fast as the British government since 1997. When I spoke to the then head of MI5 for this book, as I report in Chapter XIV, I asked him how many files they had on individuals living in Britain. 'In the low hundreds of thousands,' he replied. I wonder how many they have now.

An architect of Britain's counter-terrorism strategy, Sir David Omond, argues that to combat modern terrorism and organized crime 'intrusive methods of surveillance and investigation' will be needed, monitoring not only those suspected of committing or preparing a crime but also those not suspected of anything. All this to be done by a British bureaucracy with a spectacular track-record of both mismanaging and losing the data it collects on us.

Thirty years ago, when I went to live in East Germany, I was sure that I was travelling from a free country to an unfree one. I wanted my East German friends to enjoy more of what we had. Now they do. In fact, East Germans today have their individual privacy better protected by the state than we do in Britain. Precisely because German lawmakers and judges know what it was like to live in a Stasi state, and before that in a Nazi one, they have guarded these things more jealously than we, the British, who have taken them for granted. You value health most when you have been sick.

I say again: of course Britain is not a Stasi state. We have democratically elected representatives, independent judges and a free press, through whom and with whom these excesses can be rolled back. But if the Stasi now serves as a warning ghost, scaring us into action, it will have done some good after all.

TGA, Oxford, March 2009